TRIBAL WARFARE IN ORGANIZATIONS

TRIBAL WARFARE IN ORGANIZATIONS

PEG NEUHAUSER

BALLINGER PUBLISHING COMPANY
Cambridge, Massachusetts
A Subsidiary of Harper & Row, Publishers, Inc.

International Standard Book Number: 0-88730-355-2

Library of Congress Catalog Card Number: 88-22063

Printed in the United States of America

Library of Congress Cataloging-in-Publication Data

Neuhauser, Peg, 1950-
    Tribal warfare in organizations / Peg Neuhauser.
      p. cm.
    Bibliography: p.
    ISBN 0-88730-355-2
    1. Conflict management. I. Title.
HD42.N48 1988
658.4-dc19   88-22063
                                                         CIP

To Sharon

CONTENTS

ACKNOWLEDGMENTS

Special thanks go to all of the people who contributed their time and talent to the writing of this book. Their encouragement and involvement at each stage has been a great support to me and has enhanced the quality of both the content and delivery of these materials.

Of all the contributors, I would most like to thank Carl Selbo for his endless hours of typesetting, designing, editing and advising. Without his constant enthusiasm for this project, I might have become discouraged and given it up long ago. Because of Carl, laughter and fun were mixed in with the hard work of writing a book. Kate Spiller and Ann Marie Alderman patiently read and reread the manuscript, giving me advice that enhanced its clarity and depth.

I also thank my many clients who allowed me to learn about the tribes in their industries and who have worked so hard with me to build bridges between the tribes in their businesses. Special thanks go to Jock Whisnant and Luke Simons at J.C. Bradford and Co. investment firm, Ella Drinnon and the managers at St. Thomas Hospital, and Deborah Pugh at St. Joseph Health System. These people were often my teachers, offering some of the best examples of what an organization's tribes can accomplish when they are well managed.

I would also like to thank Vicki Watkins and her staff at the Vanderbilt University Graduate School of Management library for their research on such an unusual topic. When I explained that I wanted literature searches on tribes in organizations, they laughed and told me that was the first time they had heard that one. They took the challenge, though, and produced excellent data for me to use. Thanks also go to Patti Parnell, my assistant, who typed and proofed many versions of this work, and who has supported me at every step along the way of building my consulting business and writing this book.

Last, I would like to thank Marjorie Richman, my editor, and all of the others at Ballinger. They have been candid, sensitive, and efficient in handling my book. I have learned to appreciate the many talents that are needed to edit and publish a book.

Producing a book is a classic example of a team effort and requires the input and cooperation of many different professional tribes. It has been an honor for me to be associated with all of you.

I IDENTIFYING THE TRIBES IN YOUR ORGANIZATION

1 TRIBES IN CONFLICT
Turf Protection in Organizations

Managers spend anywhere from 25 to 60 percent of their working day dealing with conflicts or fallout from people-related problems.[1] Whenever people are gathered together to work as a group, conflict is one of the inevitable outcomes. The conflicts can range from a simple misunderstanding between colleagues about the time of a meeting to a serious battle between Sales and Production over the importance of filling a customer order for an expensive and highly customized version of a standard product. Some conflicts are nothing more than a minor irritant for the employees involved, but many of the more serious problems continue over a period of time and require a great deal of management effort to resolve. Conflict is a major source of increased stress and decreased productivity for all managers and employees in any department of any organization. It almost always ends up affecting the quality of services received by customers.

It is difficult to measure the financial cost of conflict in an organization, but it is no doubt very high. If you calculate the hourly pay for your management staff and then use the conservative 25 percent figure for the amount of time spent dealing with conflict, the yearly cost is staggering. For example, think about a medium-sized company with 1,000 employees and approximately 100 people in some kind of management role. If those managers' salaries average $40,000 a year, you have a "conflict cost" to the organization of $1 million per year. And this only accounts for management time. The cost of employee time, increased turnover rates, mistakes, and missed business opportunities would need to be factored in to come up with an accurate conflict cost. For large companies that practice "state-of-the-art" conflict—corporate politics—the cost runs far beyond 25 percent of managers' salaries.

Conflict is inevitable in any organization. But it is important that conflict be recognized and dealt with, instead of ignored and swept under the rug. Some amount of management and employee time will always need to be devoted to handling conflicts. If conflict is ignored or denied, it will fester and erupt later in much more serious ways. Then it will usually take even more time and the involvement of even more people to resolve. How much time and how effectively this time is used are the negotiable issues. Organizations that can bring various departments and specialized functions together to work as a well-functioning team do experience conflict. But they usually handle conflict in the quickest way possible, with a minimal number of people involved, and with the best outcome for the organization.

WHAT IS ALL THIS CONFLICT?

"This is a good place to work. Most of the people here know their jobs and are reasonable to work with. It's just that we've got a few difficult people around here. People whose personalities stink! If you could get rid of those people, everything would be fine."

These comments are some of the most common that are heard when employees discuss communication problems and conflict in their organizations. Marketing doesn't get along with Manufacturing. . . the nurses don't like the doctors. . . Finance can't understand why the designers will not stay on schedule and within budget. . . the marketing people insist on making promises that the service department can't deliver. . . and on and on. What is going on here? Are these problems really about personality conflicts? If they are, they are going to be very difficult to resolve. Personalities do not change easily. But there is another, more effective, solution to the problem of conflict in organizations.

Any organization with specialized functions and departments is made up of groups—which I call "tribes"— that look at their work and at the organization in very different ways. Anthropologically, these groups in organizations act very much like "real" tribes; they have their

Figure 1–1. Examples of Organizational Tribes.

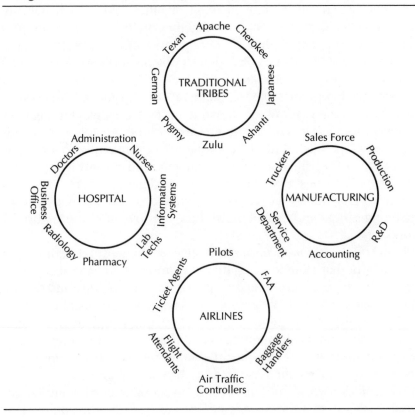

own dialects, values, histories, ways of thinking, and rules for appropriate behavior. What if we took some Apaches, Cherokees, and Pygmies, added a few Japanese and Germans—plus a Texan or two—and then said to this group, "Now go work together and get the job done!" No one would be surprised if tribal warfare broke out in this group. And yet in many ways, this is exactly what happens in most organizations today. When we create an organization or business, we pull people together from a wide range of specialities and backgrounds, put them in a building, and expect them to work together and get the job done.

Edward T. Hall, a well-known anthropologist who has written extensively on intercultural communication, tells us that each tribe or culture has its own rules that govern its thinking and behavior and that these rules usually operate at a subconscious level.[2] Psychologist and consultant Lealand Kaiser says that each individual or group has its own "reality."[3] Each tribe assumes that their "reality" is the only one or at least the only one that is right! Speaking of other tribes, each will say something like this: "Yes, I can see that they are different from us. But they aren't just different, they are wrong! And furthermore, they know that their way of doing things causes us problems, so they must be doing it on purpose to drive us nuts!"

Each tribe has predictable complaints about the others. The accounting tribe complains about the departments that are always going over budget or forgetting to fill out purchase orders before going on spending sprees. The back office operations tribe complains about departments that never fill out forms accurately and are always missing deadlines. The sales tribe complains about departments that respond slowly to customers. Each tribe is convinced that its own way of operating is right and that all those "other people" are messing up the works.

In his book, *Beyond Culture,* Hall gives a wonderful description of the opinions that members of different cultures often have about each other. He says each group takes the position of "thinking and feeling that anyone whose behavior is not predictable or is peculiar in any way is slightly out of his mind, improperly brought up, irresponsible, psychopathic, politically motivated to a point beyond redemption, or just plain inferior."[4] These are the same phrases that members of organizational tribes often use to describe each other.

"Lack of teamwork," "turf protection," the departmental "Lone Ranger syndrome"—all these terms can be used to describe the conflict that occurs between departments. I call it "tribal warfare" in organizations. Tribal warfare can take the form of all-out, open hostility between departments, with yelling and the exchange of searing memos. At other times there is no apparent conflict at all, but there is not much teamwork either. All the departments are simply ignoring each other and trying to operate as independently as possible (the Lone Ranger syndrome).

Another form of conflict is silent, behind the scenes, and more closely resembles guerrilla warfare. There is the story of the production manager who used guerrilla warfare when he received an order from Sales for 500 units of an expensive and specially designed piece of equipment. He suspected that the order was a mistake and that an extra zero had been accidentally added to the order. His guess that the order was actually for fifty items turned out to be correct. But instead of checking with Sales and correcting the mistake, he went ahead and processed the order because he did not want to pass up such a good opportunity to make the sales department look bad.[5] This is a classic case of tribal warfare.

COMMUNICATION BETWEEN THE TRIBES

There are three different patterns of communication within an organization—vertical, horizontal, and internal. (See Figure 1–2.) All three kinds of communication are important, and each must be handled well for an organization to operate effectively. Conflict and miscommunication are possible in any of the three areas. Many times there are problems in all three areas at the same time. The least studied—and in many cases the most frustrating—of the three communication patterns is horizontal communication between departments and functions.

The purpose of this book is to examine the tribal differences within organizations and to look at what happens when representatives of any

Figure 1–2.   Patterns of Communicating

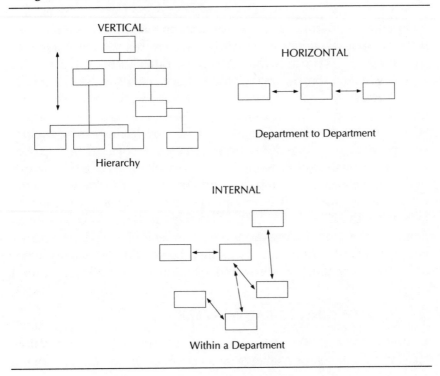

two tribes meet, try to communicate, and end up in conflict. I will describe some methods for building bridges between tribes that are useful in managing conflict, thereby reducing employee stress levels and increase the organization's productivity.

THE VALUE OF ORGANIZATIONAL TRIBES

Tribes are valuable to an organization in a number of ways. First of all, their differences can generate new ideas and innovations for your business. Each tribe looks at the products, services, and procedures of your organization from its own point of view, or "reality," and has its own ideas about how to improve or change things. If conflicts between the different points of view are well managed, a blending of these ideas can produce far better results than any one group could possibly do alone.

Tribes also offer protection against the possibility of a "group-think" syndrome taking over your company. The assumption, "We know the answer!"—or even worse, "The customer is wrong and we are right!"— is a common trap that organizations can fall into without even realizing it. Everyone sees the organization's business activity from the same point of view, so group-think becomes quite comfortable. When you have a number of tribes in your organization, however, it is difficult for this to happen. Someone is always saying, "Yes, but . . . ," or, "Have you thought of . . . ." The tribes meddle in each other's work and get in each other's way, but sometimes this interference actually helps to produce better results. The tribes, of course, have to be willing to listen to each other and to negotiate the differences, if the benefits are to occur.

Another benefit of tribes is that they foster loyalty and can be a source of high employee morale. It is fun to be a member of a tight group. You can almost always spot a team that works well together by the humor and joking among its members. The loyalty that this kind of contact often inspires can be a problem if it is strictly associated with the tribe and not with anyone else in the organization. The "us-versus-them" attitude seen in many organizations is a result of loyalties being too closely tied to the tribe. Loyalty to the tribe needs to be balanced with a clear understanding of how that tribe fits into the overall organization.

REDUCING TRIBAL WARFARE

I stood in front of 200 brokers, traders, research analysts, operations specialists, and senior managers at a securities firm's annual meeting, talking about their tribes and quoting the things they say about each other. I watched them laugh, poke each other, and jump out of their chairs to point at each other across the room as they recognized themselves and others in my descriptions. I knew I had made my point when one of the research analysts came up to me after the speech to tell me that she and one of the brokers had just run into each other, laughed together, and then agreed to go a little easier on each other back at work to see if they could build a few bridges.

A man who was a feisty defender of his tribe summed it up when he chuckled and said to me, "Now I understand why I can go to have a drink after work with that guy and we get along just fine. But the next morning at work, all it takes is one phone call and he's driving me crazy again!"

Realizing that it is a coworker's specific work behavior that irritates you, not his entire personality, is a good starting point. This book will help you go on from there to reduce your organization's tribal warfare. It is divided into several sections. Part I will describe what an organizational tribe is and how you can identify the various tribes within your own organization. A five-step assessment tool will assist you in recognizing the specific characteristics of each tribe. It is interesting to know about tribes, but what can you do about it? Part II discusses how you can create more effective and less stressful communication between your organization's tribes. Building better communication bridges gives both sides more of what they want as quickly as possible with a minimum of frustration: higher productivity and lower stress, more tribal peace and less tribal warfare.

"It has always seemed to me that the best symbol of common sense was a bridge."[6] This remark by Franklin D. Roosevelt could serve as a good motto for dealing with tribal conflict in organizations. Common sense, as most people know, often appears to be simple and straightforward on the surface, but can be difficult and complicated to maintain when you face day-to-day reality. As Robert Benchley could have been responding to FDR, "It seems to me that the most difficult part of building a bridge would be the start."[7]

Just getting started is the problem that organizations face when it comes to dealing with horizontal or tribal conflict. The challenge is to find a way to start that triggers cooperation instead of resentment and defensiveness. I have found that getting people to laugh is usually the best beginning. If you can take a serious issue and give people a view of it that makes them laugh and have fun, then it is much easier to get them to rethink the serious side of the issue as well. The questions at the end of each chapter are intended to help you take the information in this book and apply it to your own tribes. You can read this on your own, or discuss the questions with the tribes in your organization. They will help you get started in building bridges between your own tribes and in reducing your organization's potential for tribal warfare.

2 CHARACTERISTICS OF ORGANIZATIONAL TRIBES

How do you begin to identify the tribes within your own organization? You certainly know that there are differences between Engineering, Marketing, Production, Purchasing, Finance, and R&D, but how do you understand those differences in a way that will help you bring these tribes closer together and reduce conflict? There are a number of specific characteristics that you can look for to identify the different tribes. The stories employees tell, their complaints, and the things they are proud of are just some of the clues as to how each group sees itself and the organization.

This chapter will give you a brief overview of organizational tribes. In each of the next five chapters, I will then take one characteristic and explain in detail what to look for when examining organizational tribes. As you read along, it will be helpful if you keep in mind at least two groups that you are familiar with in your organization—your own department or specialty and at least one other. Often it is easier to identify another tribe's characteristics. Your own tribe is so familiar to you and so obviously "right" that it can be difficult to look at it objectively.

Each person belongs to many different tribes both at work and in their personal lives. Whenever you identify yourself with a group—"I'm an accountant," "I'm a Methodist," "These are my friends"—you are describing your membership in a tribe. This book will primarily address the tribes within organizations, which are defined by job functions or departments. But I will also discuss the informal tribes, such as friendship groups, because these tribes can have a serious impact on organizational conflict.

To begin, however, we will take a look at two broad categories of tribes common to most organizations—generalists and specialists. Specific functions or departments usually fall into one of these two categories. Sometimes an organizational conflict can be explained by simply learning that the battling groups are generalists versus specialists. Understanding the distinction between these two categories will help you to identify which departmental or functional tribes are likely to run into conflict with each other.

GENERALIST OR SPECIALIST? WHO'S WHO

Generalists and specialists work toward very different ends, have different personalities, are trained differently, and usually find each other quite irritating. They are each absolutely convinced that the other is damaging the quality of the services or products the organization delivers. As you read the descriptions of generalists and specialists, think about which tribes in your organization fall into one or the other of these categories. Some tribes will be a mixture of the two. I call these the "hybrid" tribes.

Generalists

The generalists are the people who have been hired to know a little bit about a lot of things in the organization. They have a broad range of knowledge, but not necessarily great depth of knowledge about any one area. If they are longtime employees, they may have acquired some depth of knowledge in a few specific areas. Their job descriptions, however, do not require that they develop this kind of expert knowledge, so it is usually an accident or by-product. With their broad knowledge of product lines or functions, generalists are usually the people who communicate with the outside world: with customers, clients, the public, vendors, and so on. Outsiders know even less about your organization than the generalists, who translate the organization's technical or specialized information to the layman.

Those in sales, public relations, customer relations and many senior management positions are examples of people filling the generalist role. Speed and expediency are usually very high priorities for such employees. They must often cover much ground as quickly as possible, touching on many different product lines or functions and communicating with many outside people. The sales force is, of course, a classic example of a generalist tribe. They need summarized, clear information that can be communicated easily and quickly to busy customers. They need to make sales and keep moving. From the generalists' point of view, any strategy that speeds up the process and solves their customer-based problems is appropriate

Similarly, public relations or customer relations personnel will look at everything that occurs in the organization through the eyes of the customer. Their only definitions of quality, speed, or accuracy will be the customer's definitions. "The customer is always right" is a generalist's tribal motto and translates to mean that no one's opinion matters except the customer's. For example, a computer company may have developed a new personal computer that the technicians think is a masterpiece of state-of-the art equipment, but the public either does not like it or thinks it is too expensive. The customer service people will be quick to tell you the equipment is no good, a worthless bomb. Or an airline may decide on a policy of canceling all flights that are less than 50 percent booked for financial and efficiency reasons. That airline's public relations people who have to deal with the complaints of angry customers, will tell you that their only definition of efficiency is satisfied customers arriving at their destination on time.

The three key characteristics of those in a generalists tribe are:

1. Communicating with the customers and clients and looking at products and events through their eyes
2. Having a broad range of knowledge about the company and industry in which they work
3. Having no specific expertise in one product line or technical function

Specialists

The specialists are a very different sort of tribe. They have been hired to be the experts in each of the product lines or functions of the organization. A specialist's job is to know everything there is to know about one specialized area and to stay up-to-date in that area. Most industries are changing so rapidly that the task of staying up-to-date is one of the major challenges for specialists. They usually have much less contact with the outside world and in fact are often quite annoyed if one of the generalists corners them with a client and forces them to communicate directly with him.

The specialist's job is to have depth of knowledge, not a broad range of knowledge about the company. Specialists who have been with the organization for a long time may have acquired a range of knowledge, especially if they have moved around filling different specialist roles. But a broad range of knowledge, which specialists acquire only by accident, is not a requirement of their jobs.

Some examples of those in specialist tribes are programmers, engineers, and finance, purchasing, and technical operations personnel. Manufacturing people are usually cast in specialist roles. "They are responsible for the smooth running of the factory to produce the right products in the right quantities at the right times for the right cost."[1] Their time is spent right on the factory floor, dealing with new computerized technologies, machine breakdowns, and inventory. In their opinion, the sales and marketing people live in the clouds and have very little understanding of factory economics or politics. From this specialist's point of view, marketing people "are always promising more services than can be done, coming up with inaccurate sales forecasts, and dreaming up design ideas that are difficult to manufacture."[2]

A chief financial officer in a large, nonprofit hospital described a typical specialist's dilemma. He was telling me about his frustrations with the way the word *quality* is often used by the generalist tribes in his organization. He said that these other people would arrive in his office with grand ideas for new services or for expansion of personnel or equipment, but with very few facts and figures to back up their requests for money. When he pushed them to quantify their requests, members of these tribes would usually move to their fallback position and claim that these changes were necessary to provide "quality" care. He would nod and agree that this might be the case, and would ask them to come back with figures quantifying the impact on quality. The generalists retorted that you cannot measure quality in the way the CFO was suggesting, but he claimed that you can. The battle lines were drawn between the tribes, but the conflict was already stalemated.

Figure 2–1. Characteristics of Generalists and Specialists.

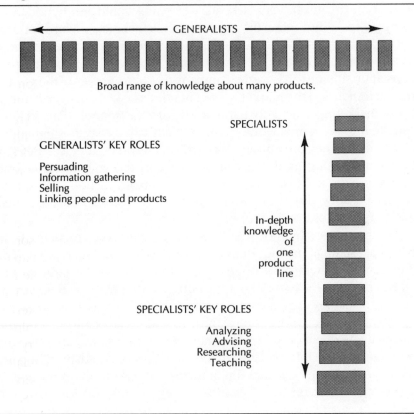

The three key characteristics of specialists are:

1. Having no primary contact with the end-user customers or clients
2. Being the company's experts in specific technical areas, functions, or skills needed to produce products and services
3. Often being unfamiliar with the activities of the organization that lie beyond their particular function

Hybrid Tribes

There are, of course, many organizational tribes that combine generalist and specialist characteristics. According to the people in these tribes, they may be generalists one minute and specialists the next. Which role they are in depends on the task they are doing or on who they are talking to. In some organizations, marketing personnel would be a hybrid tribe. They are specialists when they are using their technical skills to conduct market research, analyze statistical data, develop sales forecasts, and advise on strategic plans for the company. On the other hand, they are constantly striving to assess the company through the eyes of the public, the customer, and the markets —a generalist's task. In many organizations, marketing is actually handled by sales personnel. This kind of "marketing" personnel would be more likely to play a purely generalist role because they are entirely focused on customer contact. But any M.B.A. marketing graduate will be quick to tell you that *sales* and *marketing* are not just two words for the same function. Marketing requires a specialist orientation mixed with a customer-based, generalist perspective: a hybrid tribe.

Another set of hybrid tribes that play a key role, particularly in corporate settings, are the administrative assistants and secretaries. The importance of their role is often overlooked or ignored in large corporations because they work near the bottom of the status and power hierarchy. But they are the communication "glue" in most organizations. Assistants and secretaries control the flow and speed of information and can facilitate or cut off access. As members of tribes, they are often the best source of the informal information that flows through the company rumor mill. In one corporation, a tribe of administrative assistants is assigned to work for the sales tribe. They run information back and forth between the generalists on the sales force and the specialist tribes elsewhere in the organization, asking questions, placing orders, and fixing problems. They spend a great deal of their time talking to the specialists, especially those in the back office technical operations tribes. But the specialists in Operations are adamant that the administrative assistants are *not* specialists. These specialists complain that they often have to repeat a technical explanation five times while an administrative assistant writes it down verbatim so as to be able to repeat it later to the salesperson. If tribal warfare breaks out between the generalist and specialist tribes at a company like this, the administrative assistants and secretaries often find themselves caught in the middle. They end up getting yelled at from all sides. Managers should be concerned when this happens because these people who are catching it in the middle are key communication links within the organization. If they become alienated and decide to declare their own war against some of the other tribes, they can fairly easily slow down the information flow and sabotage the entire communication system. This hybrid tribe may be at the bottom of the organization chart, but it controls a fair amount of corporate power in any outbreak of tribal warfare.

TEAMWORK BETWEEN GENERALISTS AND SPECIALISTS

The generalist tribes and the specialist tribes need to communicate with each other frequently. The specialists provide the advice, analysis, and much of the ongoing training for the generalists. The generalists then take that information, translate it, and pass it on to the customers or the public. Neither set of tribes could function alone in an organization that has even a moderate level of complexity. But the two groups often do not work together smoothly. Below are some of the most common statements that I have heard the two groups make about each other.

Specialists' Comments About the Generalists

"The same guy will call me over and over with the same question every time it comes up on an account. What's the matter with him? Doesn't he have any memory? And if he can't remember, why doesn't he write it down?"

"They never fill out the forms correctly. They leave blanks, forget signatures, and even forget to send them in at all! Why can't they just do it right the first time and save us all a lot of time?"

"They will call me with a question, I give them an answer they don't like, so they end-run me and call my supervisor and other people until someone tells them what they want to hear. I gave them the right answer in the first place!"

"One salesman calls me to ask about a new product, so I spent time with him on the phone going over all the details. That's okay, that's my job. But then he says, 'Yeah, that sounds good. I think I want to show that to one of my clients. Now tell me all that again, and I'll write it down this time.'"

What Generalists Say About Specialists

"I am tired of being treated like I'm dumb when I call with a question. It usually isn't so much what they say, it's the tone of voice they use. By the time I hang up, I know they think I'm an idiot."

"I call to ask a simple question and want a simple answer. For example, I call a regulatory department to find out 'Can I do it?' on a particular transaction. All I want is yes or no. The customer is on the other line on hold. So what does the person on the other end do? He pulls out a letter from the regulatory agency and starts reading it to me over the phone! So I yell, 'Just tell me if I can do it!' And he yells back, 'Yes!' And we both slam down the phones."

"I see red when I hear 'Rules are rules.' That isn't an explanation, and it certainly is no help to the customer. I need to know how to get around the rules, or what alternative might work instead."

"They send me reams of paper with details about the products and services and rattle off even more details every time I talk with them on the phone. And then they wonder why I don't remember all of it. I'm not even trying to remember all those details. I figure if I need to know, I will just call them and ask. It's easier and quicker for me that way."

The us-versus-them syndrome is easy to see in these tribal comments. The tribes are not working well together. In fact, they are actually adversarial in many of these cases. When this occurs, tribes are missing the basic point of why organizations are created in the first place. To accomplish complicated tasks in the most efficient ways, "organizations" combine various groups under one roof to accomplish two things: first, *division of labor,* and second, *shared resources and interdependence.* When the collision between tribes occurs, the value of the first step, division of labor, is being emphasized, but no attention is being paid to the equally important second step, shared resources and interdependence.

In his book, *The Renewal Factor,* Bob Waterman uses the term "energy leak" to describe the time executives spend worrying about and defending against one another's "hidden agendas."[3] He says that when this is occurring among executives, it would be almost impossible for members of their groups to collaborate. If one individual works for one executive and another works for someone else, both would feel disloyal to their respective bosses or would believe that the other group is the enemy. In contrast to energy leaks leading to this kind of tribal warfare, when the different tribes learn to build bridges and to collaborate well, the organization benefits from a "gestalt" effect. The term *gestalt* means that the whole is greater than a simple summation of the separate parts. The tribes working together can produce better results than each of the individual units could do if they were all working separately—in other words, shared resources and interdependence.

Phony Teamwork

Another distinctive pattern between tribes occurs in a form subtler than the generalist versus specialist conflict. Sometimes there is the appearance of teamwork. On the surface, it appears that all the groups pull together well, are cordial and polite with each other, and are quick to offer to help when asked. They appear to be expert collaborators and to have good relationships with each other. When I interview members of these tribes, I always hear the message, "No conflict here." Tribal peace seems to reign throughout the organization. There have been times when this story has been so convincing, I am left scratching my head and wondering why the CEO is spending the time and money to bring me in to work with the organization. Then I notice a piece that does not fit with the story. Nothing ever gets done between the tribes! Not, at least, without a lot of repetitive follow-ups and nagging. Everyone nods, smiles, and agrees when they are face to face with someone from another tribe, but then they walk off down the hall and forget about what they agreed on. This is phony teamwork.

Phony teamwork is a serious energy leak. This is not tribal peace, it is silent warfare. You become aware of the battles only when you notice the absence of results. The first job is to get these tribes talking to each other about why things do not get done as promised. After peeling back a few layers, you usually find some version of us-versus-them thinking going on in all the tribes. Then you can start to build some real bridges to link the groups and move toward a form of teamwork that is more than attractive window dressing.

DESCRIBING YOUR TRIBES:
A FIVE STEP ASSESSMENT TOOL

The picture that most people conjure up when they think of an anthropologist is a Margaret Mead type in khaki clothing and hiking boots, carrying a pad of paper, a tape recorder, and a camera into the jungles to spy on remote tribes. Anthropologists then write books telling us all about how these tribes eat, work, have sex, and die. True anthropologists are probably not quite this eccentric, but they certainly are some of the best objective observers of human behavior. To understand the tribes in your organization, it is helpful to look at what is happening around you from an anthropologist's point of view. You do not have to agree with or even understand what you see. Just begin to observe; you will see that each group has its own way of thinking and acting within the organization.

The five-step assessment tool described below will help you identify the various tribes in your organization.

Step One: Listen for Language and Dialect Differences

Every industry has developed a language that is used by insiders to communicate quickly and accurately with each other. All the tribes in the organization are generally familiar with the industry lingo. New employees and the outside layman, however, have difficulty understanding most of these industry languages. One of the quickest ways to unintentionally alienate customers is to use insider's lingo that they do not understand. This language gap puts distance between you and the customer, interfering with your ability to build the kind of rapport that is needed to make the sale, explain how to use a product, or maintain a loyal, ongoing relationship.

Nontechnical retail industries have probably done the best job of dejargonizing their language for the public. In a grocery store, drugstore, or department store, most of the language used makes sense to most customers. Those in technical retail, on the other hand, usually have more complicated language and often do not make as much effort to translate for the average consumer. Car dealerships, computer equipment stores, or even the local hardware store are examples of this kind of business. Professional services groups have even more elaborate languages that confuse and intimidate the layman—medical personnel, lawyers, and psychologists, to name a few. The most elaborate languages of all probably belong to the industries or professions that have very little direct customer contact. Employees in accounting, personnel, data processing shops, production, or manufacturing primarily talk to each other, so they have the most freedom to highly develop their insider's language.

There is no doubt that these industry or professional languages interfere with the ability to communicate well with the public and the customers. The danger is that you will either leave the customer feeling stupid for not understanding or you will create the "glazed-over eyes" syndrome. When the eyes glaze over, the brain is asleep and the customer just does not care anymore! New salespeople are especially prone to drowning their potential customers in insider's language. After all, they have just finished working very hard to learn all that lingo, and they are proud of their accomplishment. Besides, they are scared and will grasp at every piece of information they know to try to make those first sales. The results are an avalanche of words pouring out at the customer, who can barely get a word in edgewise.

The problems, however, go beyond that of the industry language. If everyone in the industry always used the same language, then the only concern would be over communicating with customers and the public. But there is a second layer of language in most industries—the tribal dialects. Each department or functional area has its own dialect; sometimes different departments will even use the same words to mean different things.

For example, in a hospital the word *code* means many different things to different tribes. It can be the number entered in the computer for a test or procedure; it can be the Medicare category for a specific diagnosis; or it can mean lights flashing and buzzers going off, sending nurses and doctors racing down the hall to revive a patient who has gone into cardiac arrest. So the word that is used to determine whether you were charged accurately for those aspirin they gave you while you were in the hospital is the same word used to describe the emergency response that will determine whether you live or die within the next four or five minutes!

These dialect differences widen the gap between tribes in the same way industry language can alienate customers. New employees have to learn more than one language, and the potential for confusion or mistakes is increased. Insiders are not very likely to say to each other, "What does that word mean?" They are more likely to nod, walk away, and guess at what it means, because not understanding the dialects can mean a loss of face between tribes. Do any of these scenarios sound familiar?

Airline. Edward T. Hall notes that the language between pilots and control tower personnel is very quick, efficient, low in ambiguity or the danger of misunderstanding.[4] As long as this language is limited to use between pilots and air traffic controllers, it is very functional and it contributes to air safety. But if those tribes used the same language with other air industry tribes, or with the general public, it would probably be unintelligible to them.

Financial. In a brokerage firm, each product-line department has its own distinct dialect. A new broker who wants to sell several different products—stocks, corporate bonds, municipal bonds, retirement accounts, and so on—must learn to be multilingual. For example, in the securities industry brokers use different terms to tell different product-line departments that they are buying stocks, bonds, or funds for their clients—for instance, "circle it," "take it down firm," "made the trade."

Health care. A nurse from a home health agency told me the story of an elderly woman who called one day very upset because the agency had not "picked her up" for her doctor's appointment as promised. This was not a service normally offered, so the nurse was confused about how this arrangement had been made in the first place. She finally discovered that the agency's use of the expression "pick you up" to mean "set you up as an account with the agency" had been misinterpreted. Defining the terms did not help to calm the woman down at that point. The damage had already been done.

Step Two: Explore Differences in Values

Each tribe usually has its own set of values that underly its commitment to the work and to the tribe. Cultural tribes manifest their values most often in their religions. Although various cultures around the world have many different religious patterns, they almost all have some set of beliefs that define the meaning of life. The definitions of right and wrong—ethical standards—are usually closely associated with a culture's religious philosophy.

In organizations, "religion" takes the form of priorities, or key issues that give meaning to work: the values of the organization. When these values are clear to the employees, they will provide direction for the company. When they are not clear, you will hear comments and complaints about not knowing where the company is headed and having no guidelines or framework for making decisions. Instead, everything seems to be random guesswork or pure political maneuvering to increase power bases. Employees in an organization without a clear sense of its values will often describe themselves as pawns in the corporate power game. Morale will be low.

In organizations with a clear set of values, the majority of employees will be able to state quite easily what they are proud of about their company. They understand the organization's purpose and are clear about their role in carrying out that purpose. The direction and boundaries are clear, so that when they run into situations that require them to think on their feet to come up with quick, independent solutions, they know what to do and are confident they will be supported. Jan Carlzon, president of Scandinavian airlines and the author of the book, *Moments of Truth,* gives an excellent example of the benefits of clear values when he describes an SAS flight crew's response to a "moment of truth" situation.[5] SAS has the key values of on-time service for business travelers and a high level of customer service. (These values have been critical to the success with which Carlzon and his company have turned SAS into one of the stars of the airline industry in the past few years.) In the story he tells, an important Swedish business executive radioed ahead from his business jet, which was approaching Kennedy International Airport to let SAS know he would be a few minutes late for the flight to Stockholm. Although he did not actually say it, it was clear that he expected SAS to hold the flight. What should the crew do? In many companies this would be either a dangerous dilemma or a clear-cut decision to hold the plane and make everyone else late for this one, very important customer. For the SAS crew the guidelines, based on their values, were clear: the plane takes off on time. When the executive arrived the plane had departed, but he was greeted by an SAS official who explained that he was rebooked on a KLM flight that was leaving in thirty minutes. It was the same kind of plane, and he was booked in the same seat that he had reserved on the SAS flight. This crew obviously knew the SAS values and believed the company was serious about them.

There are overall organizational values that I call "umbrella" values. Two SAS umbrella values are on-time service and excellent customer relations. The individual tribes within an organization, however, also have their own sets of values. I call these "tribal values". Ideally, all the various tribal values can be integrated not only with each other but with the umbrella values for the organization. Unfortunately, tribal values often are not quite that clear or compatible. If you ask employees about the most important thing in their job or department, they will answer by telling you their tribal values. If you line up the answers from a number of different tribes, the potential for conflict will be obvious.

For example, ask a manufacturing company's R&D, engineering, purchasing, production, finance, credit, and marketing departments the question: What is the most important aspect of jobs in your area? Their answers will be dramatically different, and they will often be glad to tell you that those other departments are wrong and are not working for the long-term good of the company. As you can see in the examples below, when people are operating within their tribal roles, they will be remarkably consistent about their tribal values. If they believe that tribal values and umbrella values conflict, they will usually opt to follow their tribal values.

Sales.   Ask a salesperson what is the most important thing about his job. The answer will probably be something about the level of sales to the customer, or about quality of service to the accounts. The ability to provide custom orders, give special financial terms, offer easy credit, and operate within flexible budgets are usually important aspects of sales jobs.

Accounting.   Ask the same question of an accountant or chief financial officer. The answer will probably cover current, accurate records, or sound financial projections for future growth. Finance people usually talk about tight controls, tough credit terms, rational budget procedures, and standardized transactions.

R&D.   Ask an R&D technician and you will probably hear about high quality standards, adequately tested prototypes, or creative new ideas for the company. These technicians are more likely to focus on basic research that has long-term implications for the company, even if the short-term profit implications are minimal or nonexistent.

Step Three: Examine Training Differences

The training for each tribe within the organization is usually quite different. Everyone may go to the same company orientation, but that is often where similarities in training end. On-the-job training varies significantly from department to department. Each department usually has some kind of formal training that consists of either classes or learning behavior and procedures from more experienced employees. But the tribes also have an informal training, in which each new employee learns the "stories of the company." One major item on the informal training agenda is learning who the good tribes are and who the bad tribes are. Within a week or two at most, new members have learned their tribe's folklore, as well as the behavior responses that can be expected from other tribes.

There are other training and background differences between the tribes. In many industries and professions, specific formal education backgrounds are required for certain jobs—university degrees, or vocational training. There are also differences among tribes in licensing and examination procedures. These often serve as "rites of passage": passing the boards or licensing exam means you have been initiated.

Differences in training and educational backgrounds can trigger rivalries that lead to conflict. This source of tribal conflict is often the most difficult to get the tribes to talk about with each other. Often, the only way to address it is indirectly, through discussion of other characteristics, or separately—discussing it with only one tribe at a time. It is a very sensitive issue in most organizations, such as the following.

Manufacturing. In a manufacturing company there are significant differences in the training and backgrounds of the sales force, accounting personnel, product designers, service personnel, and truckers. Each group has been trained to carry out its tasks and does not necessarily appreciate the skills or complexity of the work performed by the other groups.

Hospital. In a hospital setting the physicians and nurses have clinical, medical backgrounds and hospital administrators have had business-oriented, non-clinical training focused on financial and organizational concerns. These differences often produce conflicts around issues of quality care versus financial viability.

Building Trades. Both the formal training and the informal, on-the-job (or apprentice) training of architects, contractors, and engineers are very different for these three groups. They need to work smoothly together to produce a high-quality structure for the lowest cost, but this often does not occur. They each will tell you that they have to keep a constant eye on the other two to see that they do not mess up the works completely.

Step Four: Identify the Thinking-Pattern Difference

Research from the field of psychology on how the brain functions has produced some information about the different ways in which people think or process information. This research has practical application in organizations because it sheds some light on certain kinds of communication conflicts. Some people think in more linear, logical, rational thought patterns, and others use more visual, intuitive, conceptual patterns. Figure 2–2 illustrates the four patterns that are commonly used by researchers who work in this area. The arrows pointing to the most distinctly different patterns also highlight the interactions with the greatest potential for conflict. The definitions of these patterns come primarily from the work of Ned Herrmann, who has done extensive research on thinking patterns in business settings and their impact on innovation.[6]

Tribes in organizations also tend to have distinct patterns of thinking. This does not, of course, mean that all the individuals within each tribe

Figure 2–2. Four Different Thinking Patterns.

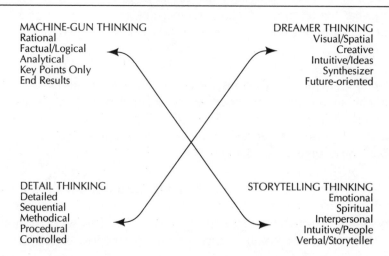

MACHINE-GUN THINKING
Rational
Factual/Logical
Analytical
Key Points Only
End Results

DREAMER THINKING
Visual/Spatial
Creative
Intuitive/Ideas
Synthesizer
Future-oriented

DETAIL THINKING
Detailed
Sequential
Methodical
Procedural
Controlled

STORYTELLING THINKING
Emotional
Spiritual
Interpersonal
Intuitive/People
Verbal/Storyteller

always use the same patterns. It is true, however, that in the work setting members of a tribe often display a remarkably consistent pattern in perceiving situations and in making decisions and judgments. There are several common ways in which this consistency is exhibited.

First of all, people with different thinking patterns will give instructions in very different ways. One person will give detailed, procedural, step-by-step instructions, writing down instructions and leaving very little to guesswork. Another kind of thinker will give a one-sentence description of the end result he wants and will often give it to you while racing by your desk on the way to someplace else. You are supposed to fill in the details yourself. If you have a meticulous, procedural thinker on the receiving end of these "on the run" instructions, that person will usually feel confused and left swinging in the breeze to make mistakes.

When it comes to making decisions, some people and tribes "run the numbers." Others use "gut feel" more often. Still other tribes report that they use a pattern that is a specific combination of numbers and hunches. The research indicates that no one of these approaches is best; if you use the approach that you are most skillful at and most comfortable with using, you are just as likely as a different kind of thinker to reach good decisions.

Two very different organizational types are the "start-up" people and the "follow-through" people. These two groups score very differently on the thinking pattern surveys, and they tend to show up in different tribes within an organization. You are much more likely to find follow-through thinkers in the engineering or quality control tribes and start-up thinkers in the entrepreneurial or artist tribes.

Step Five: Know the Tribal Rules of the Game

"Rules of the game" are the strategies or tactics used to get the job done. Another way of putting it is that the values are *why* you are doing the job and the rules are *how* you do the job. The formal rules of the company are embodied in policies and are taught to new employees in orientation sessions or employee handbooks, but these are not the rules that I am referring to here. The tribal rules are usually informal and are described better as "the way we do things around here." These rules often fall into patterns, such as the importance of speed versus the importance of accuracy. Some rules focus on customers, while others focus on operations. Listed below are a few examples of some of the rules of the game that I have heard.

"The customer is always right."	"The customer is a noisy nuisance."
"It's not in the budget, so we can't do it."	"Meet the deadline at all costs."
"Stop the production line if there is a quality problem, even if it means missing a deadline."	"Bury any failure."
"Good enough is good enough."	"If it isn't right, do it over until it is right."

Many times the rules act as mottoes for the tribe. A tribe can be known throughout an organization for repeating these mottoes with irritating regularity. More often, however, tribal rules are not so perceptible to those outside the tribe, as in the following.

Hotel.   In a hotel one of the mistakes that a manager can make is to not understand the rules of certain tribes. For example, many bellboys have two jobs: carrying out luggage for hotel guests, and doing things for the front desk such as moving guests from one room to another. They are usually tipped for the first job, but rarely for the second. For the work directly with the guests, they usually rotate like taxis waiting at a stand. A common error of hotel managers is to ask the bellboy at the front of the line to do a job for the front desk, thereby pulling him out of order and forcing him to forfeit his next tipping job.[7]

Manufacturing.   According to Phillip Kotler in his book, *Marketing Management,* if a company is "manufacturing-dominant", you will find that things are done by manufacturing's rules. The company will produce a narrow line of simply designed products, in large quantities. Sales promotions calling for quick production are kept to a minimum. Customers on back order have to be patient and wait their turn. Marketing-dominant companies, on the other hand, follow rules that favor customer responsiveness at all costs. Marketing personnel call the shots, making decisions that require Manufacturing to work overtime and to produce short runs. This results in high manufacturing costs and often results in lower quality. Kotler, of course, advocates a balance between the two tribes.[8]

Sales.   The sales force in many organizations will use a strategy for getting problems solved that I call the "multi-track rule." If a salesperson has a problem that needs to be fixed, telling one person about it and getting him to work on it is good. But telling five people about the problem and having them all working on it is five times better. The salesperson, does not, of course, tell any of the five people that four other people have been given the same mission. This technique increases the speed with which the solution is likely to be found and often produces five answers, from which the best one can be chosen.

QUESTIONS TO ASK ABOUT YOUR TRIBES

When you look at one tribe's particular language, values, backgrounds, thinking patterns, and rules of the game from within the "reality" of that tribe, these characteristics make perfect sense. But when you look at them from the perspective of one of the other tribes, they can seem irritating, disruptive, wasteful, and just plain wrong. We learned in Chapter 1 that it is a risky enterprise to try to change a tribe. If its behavior and attitudes work well for it, no tribe is likely to be motivated to change. Nevertheless, it is possible to work with the tribes so that they can see the different realities and understand how to communicate more smoothly with each other. They can be motivated to reduce the irritation inherent in conflict between tribes. That is often seen as worth the effort to learn. Besides, thinking about your organization as a cluster of tribes is funny and entertaining—another reason people are likely to be willing to give it a try.

Ask yourself the following questions to get started on identifying some of your organization's tribes.

Where are the conflicts in your organization? If managers spend an average of 25 to 60 percent of their time resolving conflicts and communication problems, you should be able to use your managers' weekly calendars as a diagnostic tool for your organization's problem spots. Which departments or functions take up a great deal of management time having their problems with other areas mediated? There will often be a predictable pattern to the problems. For example, around budgeting time the finance tribe may be in the center of a number of conflicts with other departments. Or during the peak selling season, the sales force may always be angry at everyone else in the company.

Identify a few of those "personality clashes" that occur in every organization. *Do the people who clash belong to different tribes?* If so, do those tribes have any other problems besides that of people who do not get along with each other? If you can see any pattern of possible conflict at the tribal level, then chances are you do not have a personality problem alone. Getting the clashing people to look at the organization from the other's tribal point of view may help to reduce the tension between them.

Which are the generalist tribes in your organization? Which are the specialist tribes? Remember generalists are the ones who communicate with the customers or the public directly, who are customer-oriented, and who usually have a broad range of knowledge about your company and industry. Specialists, on the other hand, are the ones who are not the primary contact for customers and who are the "experts" in a specific function or skill within the company.

Who are the hybrid tribes in your organization? Pick out one or two and think about when those tribes are required to think like generalists and when they have to think like specialists. Usually the different thinking patterns will be related to changes in the situation or to who they are talking with. If your tribe is a hybrid, are your tribe's members skillful at knowing when to switch gears? Hybrid tribes can sometimes suffer from internal problems because their members have not been adequately trained in its generalist/specialist roles and do not know where or how to switch gears.

Where are the energy leaks in your organization? Which tribes are most likely to get into battles with each other? These battles may not involve yelling or open confrontation. If inter-tribal contact causes blood pressure all around to go up, you have a mild form of tribal warfare in progress. This conflict can cause reduced productivity and lower morale and can fan the flames of negative politics in your organization—in other words, energy leaks.

Is there a pattern of phony teamwork between the tribes in your company? When asked to cooperate or to do something for another tribe, is there a lot of head nodding, smiling, and agreeing—but no results? Results are your only measure of effective teamwork. Accountability for doing what you promised to do is the heart of good teamwork. Without that, you may have a great atmosphere for the company picnic, but it is not doing much for your day-to-day productivity.

Now that you have asked yourself about phony teamwork among your tribes, ask yourself once more—am I telling the truth? This is one of the hardest questions to answer honestly. Real tribal peace comes from intertribal conflict that is negotiated well and then resolved—not from conflict that is buried.

3 TRIBAL LANGUAGES AND DIALECTS

Language is the most powerful communication tool available to humans. It can be used to link people together, push them apart, build self-esteem, destroy confidence, or give meaning to events and actions. It is so much a part of everyone's daily life that people take it for granted and lose sight of the impact that it has on how people see the world.

If you have ever been a patient in a hospital, or a family member staying with a patient, you have listened to one of the most elaborate tribal language systems that exists in any profession or industry. A common complaint about our health care system is, "They never tell you anything . . . and if they do, you can't understand what they say anyway!" A number of factors contribute to this communication gap between health care professionals and laymen, but language is definitely one of the barriers.

A discussion between a business office representative and a patient about Medicare billing procedures is often a frustrating ordeal for both parties. I have worked with groups of health care business office personnel to help them dejargonize their explanations. It is very difficult to do. Every time they come up with a new explanation, they realize that they have just substituted new jargon for the old. Their language is so full of jargon that they can barely speak when asked to talk in plain English. It is a frustrating and funny experience for most groups.

To illustrate the amount of jargon in just one profession's language, Table 3–1 is glossary of only a few of the hundreds of health care terms. They are arranged by tribe. Notice that within the hospital setting there are many different languages used between the tribes.

Table 3–1. Hospital Tribal Languages.

Medical Records	Nursing	Lab	Business Office	Emergency Room
DRGs	Acuity	Labels	Computer's down	Setup
Codes	Care plans	PCBs	Days in A/R	Pre-op
Charts	Clustering	TAT problem	EOB	STAT
Transcripts	Green Sheets	CBEs		Turnover time

JARGON

Within each industry or profession there are many dialects spoken by the various tribes. Edward T. Hall calls these different languages, "situational dialects."[1] He says that there is no such thing as a basic form of language that is universally applicable. People know many different dialects and use specific vocabularies and patterns of speech that are appropriate for different situations. The situational dialect that a person uses in his tribe at work, for example, is likely to be very different from the one that same person uses at home with the family. These situational dialects used by different tribes within the organization cause communication problems between tribes, as well as communication problems with customers and with other industries. If you have ever traveled in a foreign country where you do not speak the language, you are probably aware of the amount of extra energy it takes to try to communicate. The same kind of energy drain occurs in organizations when people struggle to understand a number of different dialects. New employees will be most aware of this extra effort as they are learning all the dialects. Veteran employees, of course, have the least problem with tribal dialects because they have been multilingual for some time and can switch back and forth quite easily. Companies with high turnover rates will suffer the most from communication confusion and conflict caused by tribal language characteristics.

"Jargon" is the common expression used to describe much of what I am referring to as tribal language. Suzette Haden Elgin, a psycholinguist who has written a series of books called, *The Gentle Art of Verbal Self-Defense,* defines jargon as "sets of words used only by a specialized group of individuals."[2] I would tighten that definition. There are two kinds of jargon, or dialects, that tribes use:

1. Words that outsiders do not understand or cannot define
2. Any words that outsiders do not normally use, even though they do know the meanings

Members of a tribe often insist that the second kind of jargon poses no problem and in fact is not jargon at all. And yet, over and over I see the use of unfamiliar language by the "experts" widening communication gaps. The jargon becomes static interference in the conversation. You can still hear what an expert is saying, but it becomes hard to pay attention to or remember what was said.

This is a common problem when experts communicate with outsiders, such as customers or vendors from other industries. For example, insiders in the computer industry are famous for their jargon terms: *hardware, software, storage, memory, bytes, disks,* and so on. Many customers who are attempting to buy equipment have a general knowledge of the terms and their definitions. But these terms are not a part of their day-to-day language, so it takes an effort to keep track of a conversation that is filled with this computer jargon—even if the customer knows the definition of every word.

Elgin goes on to specify one simple rule for using jargon: "When you are within the group to which the jargon belongs, use it; otherwise, don't."[3] Both parts of this rule are important. As a tribal member—whether you are a nurse, accountant, lawyer, secretary, or trucker—it is important that you learn your group's dialect and use it appropriately. If you do not learn to use it, you will create distance between yourself and the other members of your tribe. It is unlikely that you will ever be fully accepted by the tribe.

It is equally important, however, that you minimize the use of your tribal dialect when talking with outsiders, including the other tribes within your organization. Every time you use your dialect with another tribe, you widen the gap between the two tribes. This will make it more difficult to bridge the gap and to link your two groups together in clear and effective communications.

An example of one tribe that must routinely struggle with this language gap is the tribe of internal systems programmers. They may be assigned the task of working with a wide range of departments in their organization, designing software that will perform specific functions needed within each department. When they begin working with a new department, they try to understand its dialect well enough to interpret what the department wants from the computer so that they can design it. The department personnel often end up frustrated because the programmer "did not do what we asked for!" Part of the difficulty between these two groups is a language gap.

I once met a tribal member who was able to bridge just such a gap through her use of language. This person had worked in the information systems department of her corporation and was now in a human-resources function. She could speak both dialects. She designed what she wanted for her computerized tracking system from a human-resources perspective, but when she talked to the computer programmers she was able to "speak their language." She did not actually use the technical language of the programmers, but she was able to understand their questions about input and output and gave them the precise answers they needed—no more, no less. The programmers later commented that she was one of the best prepared and smartest people they had ever dealt with in the company. When it came time to work the bugs out of the system, she received quick and cooperative service whenever she called the programmers.

FIGHTING WORDS

I have noticed in my work that certain words between tribes have special powers. All someone has to do is say the word and the fists go up, ready for a verbal boxing match. "Fighting words" throw you off track and reduce the likelihood that you will listen effectively.[4] Instead, you will be distracted with thoughts about how irritating the speaker is and about what you are going to say back to him. The defenses are up, and the stage is set for a battle.

There are many different kinds of fighting words. A few of the ones heard over and over in many different kinds of organizations are listed on the next page. There seems to be something universally annoying about these words to certain tribes in every organization. There are, of course, many others as well.

Urgent	Hurry up	Memos
That's the rule	Forms	Quality control
Delay	Girl	In a little while
Damage	Babe	It's not my fault
As soon as I can	Paperwork	It's policy
Increasing productivity	It's not my job	The computer is down
It's not in the budget		

Certain tribes have favorite fighting words. The sales tribes are frequent users of *hurry up* and *urgent,* while back office operations will tend to opt for *that's the rule* or *in a little while.* The finance tribes, of course, are very attached to *it's not in the budget* or any variation on that theme. If there were a way to leave all the fighting words at the door when the tribes enter into negotiations or embark on problem-solving efforts, communication between the groups would be free of one unnecessary irritant. Fighting words distract everyone from the content of the discussion and set the stage for trouble between the tribes.

Aggressive language frequently begins with something like, "You people. . . ." Many times every sentence starts with "You. . . ," followed by an accusation, a judgment, or an order about what "you" should be doing. If you are attacking people instead of the issues, you are using aggressive language, which signals the other tribe to defend its turf from invasion or bullying. Usually, the members of the other tribe respond by using aggressive language themselves. I call these "verbal punches." After a round or two of punches from both sides, you have a full-blown boxing match on your hands; at best, you will end the conversation with a winner and a loser. More often than not, however, you end the conversation with two losers.

LISTENING MISTAKES

The skill of listening is essential to understanding tribal dialects. If a person tunes out and assumes he knows what the other tribe is going to say, or assumes that there is no way to understand their complicated jargon, then there is not much hope that he will be able to bridge the language gap. There are a number of common listening mistakes that people make, which interfere with their ability to translate and accurately understand another person's language.

1. Tuning out the message too quickly: People stop listening because they think the message will be too technical, too elementary, too boring, or too much like something they have heard before. This may or may not be accurate, but when you quit listening, you lose control over the conversation and take the risk of missing valuable information. This is particularly likely to occur between tribes. As soon as a member of one tribe hears the first words coming from a member of another tribe on an unwelcome topic, the tendency is to tune out. He thinks that he has heard it all before. Believing that he knows exactly what the other person is going to say, he knows exactly how he is going to answer. After all, what is the point in listening to it all again. The problem is that the other person may not say exactly what was expected. Even if he does, he is likely to end up annoyed because he senses that he is being ignored.

2. Tuning out because you do not like the speaker: The content is ignored because of who is delivering the message. The people who tune each other out are often the ones who have "personality clashes." If the dislike is even partially based on tribal differences, it would be far more helpful to "tune in" and to listen to what that other person is saying, trying to see it from his point of view. This will give you information that can be used to negotiate with that person, so that you both come away with results that are as satisfactory as possible.

3. Stereotyping the speaker: As soon as you learn what company the person is from, or which region of the country, or even which internal tribe, you assume that you have him pegged. After making a judgment about the speaker, such a listener will usually only hear the information that matches the assumptions, filtering out everything else. Often, the listener does not even know the other person, who might be an exception to the usual pattern. But this kind of listener will never know.[5]

All three of these listening mistakes increase the odds of running into problems with language differences between the tribes. Just as it takes more energy to get through the day in a foreign country where you do not speak the language because you have to listen so intensely, so it is in listening to unfamiliar tribal dialects in an organization, when you have to pay more attention to what is being said, not less attention. And yet, the natural tendency for most people is to tune out and to quit listening if the language and the information do not sound familiar.

QUESTIONS TO ASK ABOUT TRIBAL LANGUAGE

When members of the tribe are gathered together talking about work, what are the typical topics discussed? List as many topics as you can. Take each one of those topics and repeat a few sentences of what the tribal members might say about it. These sentences are likely to be filled with jargon or tribal dialect.

What is the jargon used in your tribe? Remember that jargon is defined as: (1) words that outsiders do not understand or cannot define; and (2) any words that outsiders know the meanings of, but do not use routinely. List as many words as you can think of under each of these definitions. Now try to think of substitute words your tribe could use that customers, outsiders, or other organizational tribes would understand more easily.

Develop your own tribal glossary. Make a list of all the words, expressions, jokes, mottoes, and so on that you can think of for your tribe. Define each word using only nonjargon language.

Identify as many fighting words as you can for each tribe. *What are your complaints about the other tribes?* If you start talking about all the things you wish those other people would do differently, you are likely to mention a few of the fighting words in your descriptions. Look over the list of examples given in this chapter, and add more of your own.

Which listening mistakes are you most likely to make?

1. Tuning out the message too quickly because it is too complicated, too simple, too boring, or too familiar: Identify who tends to trigger this reaction in you. Are they people from other tribes?
2. Tuning out because you do not like the speaker: Think of several people in your organization who you do not like and recall the last conversations that you had with them. Can you remember the topic of that conversation and what those people said?
3. Tuning out by stereotyping the speaker: Think of several of the other tribes that are difficult for your tribe to work with. Are they the people who you are most likely to tune out? Do you assume that new people joining that tribe will be just like all the rest?

   This may be a hard question to answer honestly about yourself or your own tribe. If you are willing to ask, the other tribes who work with your groups on a regular basis can probably tell you which of these traps you tend to fall into.

What can you do to stop making these listening mistakes? After you
have identified several of the situations in which you are likely to stop
listening, think about what you might be able to do to increase the
likelihood that you will listen next time. Take notes if it is a phone
conversation; repeat key points that the other person makes, for
clarification; or look straight into their eyes when they are talking. Find
some way that works for you to get yourself to concentrate on what the
other person is saying.

How often do you use the word you *to start your sentences when you
are in a problem or conflict situation?* If you use this word often,
chances are that you are using aggressive language. *You* is usually
followed by an accusation, or blame, or an order to act. These statements will often trigger tribal warfare. Try to switch the focus; start your
sentences with *I* and then state what you want or what you think about
the situation. But watch out: You may find yourself saying, "I think that
you are an uncooperative S.O.B. and should be eliminated from the
company, etc. . . ." Obviously, this is still aggressive language.

It is not realistic, in my opinion, to expect tribes within an organization to weed out all their tribal jargon in conversations with each other.
It is too much trouble. But it is important to be aware that these dialects
are a barrier. When the inevitable miscommunications do occur, it does
not necessarily mean that someone was not listening, or is just plain
stupid! Bilingual communication is always difficult.

4 TRIBAL VALUES

A discussion of values within an organization can take many different directions. Individual employees have their personal values that they bring with them to work; the tribes have their own values that represent their priorities; and the organization has umbrella values that underly the company's mission. Ideally, these three sets of values are coordinated. Unfortunately, they often are not, and this leads to confusion and conflict between the tribes, as well as to a lack of clear direction or pride in the company. In his book, *Peak Performers,* Charles Garfield uses the term "alignment" to describe the ideal state in an organization: when employees feel that "contributing to the organization directly contributes to their personal mission—values in sync."[1]

Conflict between personal, tribal, and organizational values is a drain on the motivation and energy of the entire organization. Energy is spent either arguing about priorities or, even worse, not arguing at all—individuals and groups just going off in their own directions, setting independent priorities and following their own missions. When tribes or individuals routinely work along their own independent paths, the atmosphere of the organization is usually very political, in the worst sense of the word. In a setting where everyone is "out for themselves," each tribe knows that it needs to gather as much power as possible and must keep most of its agenda hidden, to be able to accomplish its mission. In values-driven organizations, however, tribes and individuals still want power but they get it through collaboration and working in sync with others. They gain their power and influence through performance.

When an organization focuses on teamwork and its umbrella values, there will be events and behaviors that make that commitment obvious to outsiders as well as to the organizational tribes. For example, in one organization that has about 1,500 employees and between thirty and forty distinct tribes, a departmental awards program has been initiated. Individual employees or departments can nominate another department for the award, citing specific examples of that department's outstanding performance. A department is not limited as to the number of times it can win the award. This organization takes the attitude that if one group is nominated and wins four times in a row, then more power to it. Peak performances, enhanced by collaboration and teamwork, are what makes you a winner in that organization.

Values are the primary source of enthusiasm and motivation for most people. As many studies have shown, money is also an important motivator, but can never make up for a lack of pride or a sense of meaning from the work. One manager in a construction company told me how she is always a little surprised at the reaction of the craftsman tribes when they have to do a job over again because it either did not satisfy the customer or did not meet company standards. She sees this as a perfect opportunity for this tribe to make twice the salary for one job. "But do they go willingly, focusing on this opportunity to make more money? No! You have impinged on their sense of pride in their work! You have damaged their view of themselves as good and competent craftsmen." Pride in the quality of their work is a theme you hear when tribes are talking about their values. At times it even seems to outweigh the value of extra money that could be earned.

Robert Waterman gives a number of examples of organizations that seem to run on "causes."[2] He says that quality is the most common cause and cites companies such as Maytag and Hewlett–Packard for their long history of focusing on quality. He goes on to describe Ford's umbrella values (or causes) as employee involvement, quality products, and a customer focus. Club Med's cause is described as making each person's vacation "an antidote to civilization." Dana Corporation focuses on "productive people" and has recently added a new emphasis on being "market-driven".[3] All these organizations are making an effort to commit to clan values that their tribes and employees can rally around. In these companies, the individual, the tribe, and the organization are in sync when it comes to values. There is nothing simple or easy about becoming a values-driven company. It takes consistent, long-term effort from all employees. But as many U.S. companies have demonstrated, it can be done, and values can be maintained over a long period of time.

IDENTIFYING INDIVIDUAL VALUES

Because every tribe is made up of individuals who bring their own personal values to the workplace, it is important to recognize the significant impact of these personal values on the organization. The umbrella values that an organization chooses to adopt are usually the personal values of a few individuals such as the founder, or the associates who helped to start the business. The organizations that are most successful at maintaining a focus on their umbrella values over a long period of time are usually the ones that have managed to consistently select new leaders who are personally committed to the same values as those of the organization. IBM is the classic example of an organization that has been able to maintain its founder's focus on quality and service. There are hundreds of stories about IBM management's commitment to these values.

In many cases, however, the focus on umbrella values fades quickly when the founder dies or sells the business. The business may continue to survive, but never at the same level of excellence or with that sense of synchronization between individual, tribal, and umbrella values. One company's founder was legendary for his commitment to humanitarian values and to an entrepreneurial, competitive spirit, but there was a significant shift in the company's values after his retirement. He was still a legend, but only as a memory. There was no one of his stature to step in and take his place. The entrepreneurial, competitive spirit disintegrated into divisional empire-building as senior officers fought for more turf and more power. The humanitarian values took a back seat to bottom-line concerns and to corporate growth. For many of the employees who were personally committed to those humanitarian values, the result of these changes was that they lost all reason for working hard. Growth and profits did not mean as much when there were no clear-cut values of caring and quality service to strive for at the same time. The turnover rate at this company shot up rapidly at that point.

Identifying personal values is very easy for some people because their family or religious backgrounds have always helped to clarify these values. Many people, however, have difficulty identifying their specific values. Often the easiest way to identify a few of your key values is to look back over your life and identify those peak experiences when you experienced some event that left you feeling satisfied or rewarded. If you are trying to identify work-related values, it is most useful to think of peak events or experiences in work settings. After several of these experiences have been identified, you can look over your list and answer the question: What was it about those events that was inspiring, motivating, exciting, or satisfying? Often certain words or phrases will repeatedly come to mind. These usually represent at least a partial description of your personal values.

For example, one corporate manager cited her peak experiences in work settings as taking a new job she knew nothing about, but then doing it well; successfully starting a new function from scratch; and coaching several employees in career growth and then watching them receive promotions and honors. When she asked herself why these events were her peak experiences, two themes emerged: the thrill of taking risks that pay off, and the satisfaction of warm, loyal relationships with colleagues. These answers represented at least two of her key personal values and indicated the kind of tribe and the kind of company that she needed to work for if she was to be satisfied.

IDENTIFYING TRIBAL VALUES

As with individuals, listening to the members of a specific tribe tell stories about the tribe's "finest moments" will tell you a great deal about their tribal values. Accounting departments tell the story about the payroll run that blew, but everyone pitched in and stayed until three in the morning to get the checks out on time the next day. Or customer service tribes will tell the story about taking a midnight trip on the back roads of some rural state to deliver an order that had been delayed. R&D people talk about the times when they managed to take a failure on one product and turn it into a successful idea for a completely new product that made the company a lot of money. Such stories contain the themes of tribal values—accurate and timely work, customer satisfaction, and innovation.

One way to identify a tribe's values is to ask some of its members to name two or three of the most important things about their work in the tribe. Or have them define what quality means within their tribe. Get them to tell you what they are proud of about their work. If it is a tribe with low morale, get its members to tell you what they wish they could be proud of. Ask them if the organization would be in trouble without them, and then listen to the stories about what would go wrong or would not be done properly. When one tribe says that it has to keep an eye on other tribes so that they will not mess up the works, ask that tribe what it means by that. What does "messing up the works" mean to each tribe? You will rarely hear the same description from any two tribes. As you listen, write down the key words that you hear in each description or response. You will collect many different words and phrases, but there will probably be a pattern that you can condense into a few key phrases, which will describe some of the tribe's most important values.

Each tribe's key values describe the most important aspects of its work. Each tribe was created to provide some specific form of added value to the organization. The members of each tribe are trained to carry out specific functions within the organization, although these functions and their purpose often appear to contradict the functions and purposes of other tribes. Keeping costs under control may be one of the finance tribe's key values, but Engineering is focused on the development of new products that require long lead times and somewhat unpredictable schedules and costs. At the same time, Sales is focused on moving products out into the market as fast as possible; cost, adequate design, and testing time are not the sales tribe's highest priorities or values.

If you asked these three tribes what is good for the organization, they would each give you a different answer. These tribes are also likely to tell you that they have to "keep an eye" on the other groups, which might otherwise use poor judgment, emphasize the wrong priorities, and damage the organization. By defending its own tribal values, each tribe sees itself as protecting the organization, while it carries out its own functions in a high-quality manner.

In my experience, tribes are more humorless about their values than about any of their other tribal characteristics. If these values are threatened (or are perceived to be threatened), tribal members often react intensely and emotionally. If you keep in mind that these values represent their sense of purpose, satisfaction, and pride in their work, this defensive reaction makes sense. Trying to change their values or eliminate old values that are no longer appropriate can be a trigger for revolt—resulting in high turnover, unionization, low morale, and loss of productivity. Any change in tribal values would ideally be a gradual process, with the members themselves highly involved. If this is not possible, it is important to at least be sensitive to the very real pain and upheaval associated with organizational or industrial changes that require a shift in values.

Nurses, for example, are one of the largest tribes in health care settings, and they usually cite personal, hands-on care for patients as one of their key values. In the past few years, the health care industry has changed dramatically, shifting toward increased competition and greater concern for cost reductions and streamlined services. Many nurses see these changes affecting staffing levels and sharpening financial constraints and conclude that their key value of personal, hands-on patient care is being deemphasized and threatened. If they believe that these changes threaten their key values, they can be counted on for an angry and impassioned response. If their concerns about values are not adequately addressed, they lose their sense of purpose and motivation. When this happens, they often burn out and eventually may even leave the profession. Although the response of nurses to changes in the health care industry is an unusually strong example of a reaction to a threat against tribal values, this type of response is typical of most tribes.

IDENTIFYING UMBRELLA VALUES

The umbrella values of the organization can often provide a way to link the individual and tribal values. If you can step back and see the big picture, all the pieces may fit together better than you realized they would. Moreover, umbrella values can be seen in any organization, reflected in its most important beliefs about itself. What do its employees say they are proud of about the company? What are the organizationwide legends? They may be exaggerated, but no one cares. The points behind the stories are true.

Tom Peters tells a story that illustrates well one of IBM's companywide umbrella values. There was an IBM system crash at a major client facility shortly before Tom Watson, the IBM CEO, was scheduled to meet with the client company's president at that facility. A team of IBM technicians left on a midnight bus ride through the hills of West Virginia to get there as quickly as possible to fix the system before Watson arrived. They drove through blinding rain over winding mountain roads and arrived at 4:00 a.m. Watson's executive assistant had already arrived and was waiting to greet them. No one could imagine where he had come from or how he had gotten there so quickly, but somehow he had done it.

IBM's umbrella values of quality service, quick response time, risk-taking, and extraordinary efforts are all apparent in this story. The technicians went to great lengths to be sure Watson had something to be proud of when he arrived at that company to meet its president. Any longtime IBMer can entertain you with hours of similar stories that represent their umbrella values—"It's the IBM way."[4]

Umbrella values are the guidelines for an organization's tribes and individual employees to follow. If they are effectively communicated and widely believed by the employees, these values will tell you two things:

1. What direction everyone in the company is headed in. Is it pleasing the customer at all costs, shutting down the product line to correct quality defects, or advertising your design failures so that someone else can turn them into a success in some other way? If you know the direction, then you can use your own judgment to handle specific problems or make specific decisions.

Jan Carlzon tells of an SAS flight attendant's ability to make this kind of judgment call when she was faced with a problem. An SAS flight had fallen behind schedule because of a snowstorm. Two of the company's most important umbrella values are on-time schedules and high levels of customer service. So the flight attendant decided to offer everyone free coffee and biscuits to compensate for the delay. She needed to order extra servings, so she went to the catering supervisor to place the order. This person turned her down because extra servings were against regulations. Following regulations at all costs is *not* an SAS umbrella value, and the flight attendant knew it. She saw a Finnair plane docked at the next gate and remembered that Finnair was an external customer for the SAS catering service. Finnair was not bound by the same regulations as SAS employees. The flight attendant found a Finnair colleague and had him order the extra servings she needed. When they were delivered, she used SAS petty cash to buy them and proceeded to serve the snacks to her passengers. Carlzon describes this incident with pride as a classic SAS "moment of truth."[5]

2. What boundaries everyone must work within. These limits are usually set by a company's tactics, budget, or quality specifications. If the limits are too narrowly defined, however, the front-line employees and supervisors lose their ability to make decisions quickly and effectively—their hands are tied. Waterman describes the ideal boundaries as those that provide a broad "solution space."[6] That is, the employee handling a problem or making a decision has a wide range of options, within clear guidelines or limits. "Rules are rules" would not make sense in a company whose employees have enough solution space, or autonomy, to make decisions and adjustments as needed. For example, if a company has rules that the billing department is supposed to follow about credit limits, thirty-day payment cycles, and front-end deposits, boundaries would be defined by how flexible these rules were. Are they "the law" with no exceptions, or can a billing clerk make autonomous decisions based on the circumstances of a particular account, using these rules as guidelines? If the company has a key value of customer satisfaction, the billing department may have been given a clear mission to be not only efficient in their billing and collection efforts but responsive to customer needs. Not all accounts would be handled in exactly the same way, but the rules would still be used as consistent guidelines for making decisions.

Direction and boundaries combine to make up an organization's umbrella values. But many companies have serious problems with direction and boundaries. Changes in top management or major changes within the industry or marketplace can cause a crisis in values. Top-management changes alone can trigger a change in either direction or boundaries. Direction changes when the umbrella values shift—moving away, for instance, from responsive customer service to an emphasis on efficient, streamlined manufacturing procedures. A change in boundaries can occur when the enforcement of rules or policies becomes either tighter or looser than before. Lower levels of management and front-line employees are often left confused by these changes if their implications are not clearly spelled out and repeated frequently during the transition time.

The tribal values are usually not affected as much as the umbrella values when such changes occur. The tribes move along doing what they have always been doing. But employees may feel lost, or like they are working in a vacuum. "I don't know where we are going anymore" is a statement heard over and over in companies that have lost their sense of direction. "I spend all my time defending my department's turf" is a statement heard when the boundaries are unclear. The tribes often continue to do the best they can, but the "glue" is missing. Nothing is holding the company together.

One kind of boundary, ethical standards, gives rise to some of the most serious problems of all in many organizations. Companies have elaborate written codes of behavior, but employees often see them as no more than window dressing. The codes may be good public relations, but they do not serve as effective boundaries or guidelines for employee behavior. But if a company does not have some other way of clearly transmitting its ethical standards—or if it really has no such standards—employees may experience conflict with their personal beliefs. Their own ethical standards do not match the company standards of behavior. If there is an "ethics gap" for a large number of employees, they will be very unlikely to take any of the organization's umbrella values seriously. Commitment is replaced with cynicism and low morale. In short, it is hard to find much to be truly proud of about the organization where they work.

CLASSIC UMBRELLA VALUES

There are a number of umbrella values that are present in many companies. Many others are more specific to a particular industry or company, but the following provide a good starting point for identifying your own organization's umbrella values.

Customer Satisfaction

Satisfying the customer is the number-one umbrella value for many organizations, not just for their sales forces. IBM's service record and Proctor and Gamble's 800 number printed on every product it sells are examples of the customer service in companies whose behavior matches their commitment to their customers. When a customer-driven company defines quality, it looks to its customers to hear what quality means to them. Its boundaries include flexibility in the rules when it comes to the customer's needs, but clear limits on any behaviors that would be damaging to its relationship with its customers or clients.

Innovative Products and Services

Creativity that translates into practical products and services is another umbrella value in many organizations. The increasing pace of change in our society makes the ability to innovate a necessity. 3M is probably the most famous company in the world when it comes to innovation. Art Fry, the inventor of the now famous Post-It Notes has become legendary beyond the borders of 3M. Those little pads of sticky paper are now as much a part of standard office supplies as staplers and ball point pens. The Art Fry-3M story represents the best combination of perseverance, guts, and creativity. But any innovation-driven company that encourages its employees' commitment to developing new ideas and products can have its own versions of Art Fry.

Employee Involvement

In some companies, employee involvement is a way of life, not just a strategy to be used for occasional projects. The opposite umbrella value is held by those companies where managers distance themselves from the products and from the producers of those products, becoming professional managers and experts in specific functions such as financial analysis or marketing. To managers in this setting, it makes very little difference whether the company produces toys or paper products; in either event, human resources are simply an expense to be minimized.[7]

Contrast that situation to "management by wandering around," which is so commonly discussed in business these days. Peripatetic managers know employees personally and are familiar with what goes on in their departments or functional areas. One of the main reasons that this approach works is because it allows employees to know senior management and to have input. It sets the stage for groups or individuals to have access to management when needed. In one hospital, the CEO was famous for actions like showing up at two in the morning to chat with the night staff, or arriving early to "help" in the kitchen, flipping pancakes and serving the eggs and bacon to employees who came through the line. When he called a group of employees together to work on a problem, they always believed he was serious and sincere.

Willingness to Take Risks

Some companies put a high value on taking risks. This predilection is often closely linked to innovation. There is usually a great deal of laughing, teasing, practical joking, and storytelling in these companies. But when the going gets rough, they switch from humor to intense concentration and extraordinary efforts to get the job done.

Steve Jobs leading the product development teams at Apple Computer in intense and exhausting efforts to "do the impossible" is an example of this umbrella value in action. Charles Garfield describes his first job working on the first manned spacecraft back in 1967. "Going to work there every morning was like signing up for one of the greatest adventures on Earth."[8] No one needed to tell the employees working on that project that they were involved in a technological challenge unlike anything the United States had taken on before. The lives of astronauts and the prestige of the country were depending on their success. Garfield reports that the performance levels of most employees in his company soared to levels above anything anyone had predicted before the project. Taking risks to achieve ambitious goals may well be one of the greatest human motivators of all.

Teamwork

Teamwork is the way people work together within the tribe, between tribes, or even with outsiders such as suppliers, vendors, or customers. Words such as *trust* and *integrity* are often heard at companies with a strong emphasis on teamwork.[9] Contrary to popular opinion, research indicates that cooperation is much more effective than competition for increasing productivity and quality.

Nearly every study contrasting competitive efforts with cooperative efforts has demonstrated that cooperation produces better results. According to Alfie Kohn, author of *No Contest*, success often depends on sharing resources.[10] But resources cannot be shared effectively if individuals or tribes are pitted against each other. Space, skills, budgets, equipment, and time are all resources that can be hoarded or shared, depending on whether teamwork is seen as an important value within the organization. To the organization that value teamwork, the hero is often the team, not individuals. The emphasis is on relationships between people and on a network of contacts.

One manager in a large company known for its high level of negative politics managed for a while to create an "island" of teamwork among her direct reports. They met regularly to critique each other's projects, offer support and resources, and maintain a clear sense of direction for their own team. The message from the manager was, "You can say anything you want inside this group, air your complaints, argue, or question our decisions. But when we walk out that door and face the rest of the company, the motto is, 'Everything is fine.' We are a tight team that *never* double-crosses or battles with each other in public." That team outperformed every other team in its division on number of projects completed, quality of work, and on-time, under-budget delivery. The team's morale was high and turnover was nonexistent.

Unfortunately, this kind of success cannot usually be sustained if it comes from only an island of teamwork. It is built too much on individual personalities and values, not on organizational umbrella value of teamwork. When this manager moved on to another position and the team members scattered throughout the company, they found no other such teams to join.

High Quality

High quality is the most commonly cited umbrella value for most companies. It is such a general term that it is almost meaningless until you define it specifically for your industry and organization. Employees have to know their company's definition of quality. They have to be able to see the lack of quality when it exists and know how to correct it. But most importantly, employees must be given a *consistent* definition of quality, so that they are all working by approximately the same standards. This consistency can apply to everything from the repair and service track record on major product lines to whether letters are allowed to go out with typos and misspellings. *Quality* is a glamour term, but making it a reality takes a lot of detailed, tedious, persistent hard work.

According to Tom Peters, quality is not a technique, it's an attitude, a "passion."[11] He tells about getting upset during a lecture by a Hewlett-Packard executive on the subject of quality circles. Peters disagreed with this executive's emphasis on a management technique as the "answer." In his opinion, Hewlett-Packard was founded on a "bone-deep belief in the ability of *everybody* in the organization to contribute creatively to the betterment of the quality of the products. Given that bedrock, getting HP's quality circles to work was like falling off a log."[12] He goes on to praise the executives and the company, not for its techniques, but for its management commitment to its employees and its products. The umbrella value of producing high-quality products is what makes Hewlett-Packard successful in Peters' opinion, not a particular technique such as quality circles. In a company that did not have a history of valuing quality, quality circles would be likely to fail.

LINKING UMBRELLA VALUES TO TRIBAL VALUES

Once you identify several of your organizational umbrella values, the next step is to look for ways to link them to tribal values in a meaningful, practical way. I am not talking about hanging the mission statement in everyone's office. There is nothing wrong with doing that, but it does not bring those values to life or give them practical meaning for your tribes or individual employees. There are many ways to impart umbrella values to the tribes to bring them closer together. I will make some suggestions, but it is really necessary for you to think about your own values and for you and your company to come up with ideas that make sense in your situation.

There is one general principle to keep in mind when deciding on the best way to link tribal values to umbrella values. Each tribe must personally participate in carrying them out. Values cannot be just an idea, or something that other people do. Ideally, each individual participates in carrying out the values, but this is not always possible. If each tribe, however, has some role in making these values a reality in the organization, tribal and umbrella values are much more likely to be successfully linked.

If being close to the customer is identified as an umbrella value, then strategies for bringing that value to life for each tribe will probably include their seeing and talking with the customers. You can talk about customers and their needs constantly, but until the tribes meet and know real human beings and listen to what they have to say, it is all just theory. Your back office tribes, technical tribes, operations tribes, all need to hear directly from the customers what products or services they need and how they want them delivered. This contact does not work as a one-shot effort. It has to become a routine part of each tribe's responsibilities and should be considered in job descriptions, evaluations, and reward systems. If tribe-customer contact happens in the way I describe here, there will automatically be less conflict between those tribes with high customer contact and those with less contact. You will narrow the gap between these two kinds of tribes. The difference is still there, and negotiation will still be necessary; but it will be easier, with an activated umbrella value, to bring them together.

If innovation is one of your umbrella values, then each tribe needs to have a piece of the innovation action. *Innovation* is a broad, vague term, and there are many ways to define it. Each tribe may have a different definition, but still understand that their definition is encompassed by the company's. For R&D it may mean new designs or products. For the truckers it may mean a new idea for protective packaging, or better coordination between the delivery and installation tribes. Ask yourself these questions: Are new ideas that improve operations defined in your company as innovation? Do your company's tribes have some channel for getting their ideas implemented? Does anyone ask for their ideas on a regular basis? Can they try out their ideas on their own without four layers of bureaucratic approval? Are they rewarded for their innovations?

When I go into companies to work on innovation issues, I often hear senior management saying that innovation is an umbrella value. I then talk to frontline employees, when I ask about their role in innovation, they either give me blank stares or laugh and say, "Are you kidding? Nobody wants to hear and besides, who has time anyway?"

If your values are "alive," a reasonable number of members from each tribe will go home at night knowing that something they did that day was directly tied to some of your company's umbrella values. They will also find that it usually takes cooperation between tribes to be successful at carrying out those values. Umbrella values almost never stay within the boundaries of one tribe.

WHEN VALUES CHANGE

Managing new or changing values is a necessary skill for most organizations. In the health care industry, the umbrella value of satisfying the customer was nonexistent as little as five years ago. Increased competition and the end of cost-based reimbursement ("spend more-make more" in government reimbursements) changed all that. Now patients are no longer seen as passive recipients of care who should keep quiet and let the medical team do its work, nor are the families seen as noisy nuisances. Patients and their families are now viewed as customers with buying power and many options for receiving health care. Not liking the way they are treated is one of the most common reasons people now give for why they changed doctors, clinics, or hospitals. Billboards and radio commercials send the public various "we care" messages from competing health care providers. But when a patient or family member actually enters a doctor's office, a clinic or a hospital, can that person *tell* that the medical staff now cares? Many people will be quick to tell you that the main change so far in health care is the advertising, that the attitudes have not caught up. Although this is not a fair or accurate assessment of all clinics and hospitals, it is a good indication that values really did change slowly at some clinics and hospitals, if at all.

To evaluate changing values in your own organization, identify which values are (1) current values actually being carried out in the day-to-day behavior of management and employees, and which ones are (2) "wished-for values" that need to be in place and may even be written down, but are not evident in anyone's day-to-day behavior. In other words, decide first what you *are* proud of about your organization, and secondly, what you *wish* you could be proud of. If you kid yourself into believing that the second set of wished-for values really do exist, then you will do nothing to make them a reality. You will maintain a cynical environment where everyone will be inclined to fall back on their own, more stable tribal values to guide their behavior, in the absence of any way to link values with other tribes for the common good of the company.

Turning the wished-for values into current values is usually a slow process. Some researchers believe that it is best to start on a small scale, with limited employee participation.[13] They say that this allows you to choose participants whose beliefs and values are in line with the changes and that the changes can thus be treated as a pilot project, making it easier to correct mistakes with a minimum of embarrassment. Many people insist that it is possible to take a broad, systemwide approach to a values change and make much faster progress.

I have seen both approaches work, but I have one warning if you decide to go for fast-paced, sweeping change: you *must* have top-management support. In fact, *support* is too weak a word for what is required. You must have top-management passion for and obsession with the change. The CEO and senior management team must lead and inspire an organization into rapid values changes. I am not talking about flashy personalities and melodrama. I am talking about leadership that is clear, sincere, and present everywhere in the organization. This commitment cannot be temporary; employees and tribes have to realize that this one is for keeps. Some will follow the changes with enthusiasm and others will follow grudgingly—but everyone needs to know that they must follow. When you are talking about changing organizationwide values, all the tribes must cooperate. And that takes committed leadership which will put its time and efforts behind the new values.

SYMBOLS

Symbols that represent values, both tribal and umbrella, are important to an organization trying to communicate those values. They teach new employees what the values are, signal changes, or protect current values. Symbols are useless, or even harmful, if they are not based on sincere values. You can never use a symbol as a substitute for commitment to a value.

The umbrella values of an organization can be symbolized in many ways. On the corporate grounds of a Catholic health care facility, thousands of well-tended rose bushes and a statue of the founding sisters are powerful reminders of the religious order's umbrella values of caring, growth, and sisterhood. CEOs in some companies forgo the fancy penthouse offices and work in the middle of the action where they can see everything around them and be seen. Their desks (or lack of them) become a powerful symbol for their management style.

One kind of symbol can be particularly useful for rallying the tribes together into a united front. I call it the "brand X" symbol: The Competition. Many organizations use their competition to trigger an enthusiastic, fighting spirit among their tribes. A few years ago I did some work with a retail company in a fairly small town. The managers in this facility had one of the tightest teams I have ever seen in an organization. They were funny, feisty, and creative in their continual discussions about how to outsmart "brand X," their name for their main competitor in town. During the time I worked with that group, I never did learn the name of the other company. "Brand X" was the only answer I ever got to questions about its real name. When threatened by something or someone from the outside, most groups will band together to protect their own. If managed well, this kind of symbolism can be an excellent way to foster greater teamwork.

Tribal values can be symbolized in similar ways, even though the symbolic stories or events are confined to a particular segment of the organization. For example, a production manager who was having quality problems on the line used the symbolic power of traffic lights in his efforts to improve the situation. He installed them in the factory and programmed them to turn red whenever quality dropped below a certain level. Assembly lines were shut down and would not start up again until the problems were corrected.[14]

Some tribes have certain rituals—such as lunch together on a regular basis, or celebrations of birthdays and other events—that become symbols of their teamwork and communication. In other tribes the work schedule can be a tribal symbol related to quality, embodying the push to be the first with the best. People come in early, stay late, or work on Saturdays. In addition to the added productivity, this extra effort is symbolic of tribal commitment to individual projects.

If the tribal values are linked to the organization's umbrella values, then all these symbols will reinforce each other. But as with any tribal behavior, if tribal and organizational values do not mesh, then tribal symbols will not blend well with either those of other tribes or those of the organization. The symbols are no more than a barometer of the values that are operating in an organization. They are important only because they are an easy way for employees and outsiders to see the values in action.

QUESTIONS TO ASK ABOUT YOUR TRIBAL VALUES

What have been some of your peak experiences in your working career? They may have been at your current job or at previous jobs. Try to think of at least three or four experiences that were extremely satisfying, challenging, exciting, or rewarding in some way. List as many as you can.

Why were those events peak experiences for you? Look over your answers to the question above and, for each one, summarize what it was that gave you satisfaction. What are the common themes? Do you like risk? Is it relationships that are important? Do innovation and change excite you? Or do you prefer the challenge of solving difficult problems? Your answers may not be as eloquently stated as your organization's values and philosophy, but that is not important. What is important is that you gain some idea of what you value. The value you find in your work is what motivates you and will continue to give you a sense of satisfaction.

What are the two or three most important things about the job your tribe performs for the organization? If your tribe was taken away, what tasks or functions would not be done, or at least not done well?

How do you define quality *within your tribe?* Be as specific as you can. What acts or performance levels are, for your tribe, examples of outstanding quality?

What was your tribe hired to do? What is the "mission" for your tribe? What is the added value that your tribe brings to your organization?

What are you proud of about your tribe? What do you wish you could be proud of?

Look at your organization's favorite stories and folklore. Researchers in organizational culture often use these as one of their best tools to identify a culture's umbrella values. *What are the stories about, who are the heros, what is reverent or irreverent?*

Which of these umbrella values that are common in other organizations seem to fit your company?

- Being close to the customer

- Innovation to keep pace with rapid change

- Employee involvement—staying close to the people who produce your goods and services

- Teamwork and trust between individuals and groups

- Adventure and risk-taking

- Quality (does your organization have its own definition?)

Steve Brandt, author of *Entrepreneuring in Established Companies* describes an exercise done at the Stanford Graduate School of Business with a group of corporate managers.[15]   They are asked to picture themselves stranded on an island in the South Seas with the entire officer corps of their company. They know rescue is on the way, but it will be ninety days before they will be picked up. They have several minutes of battery power left on a radio, and they are asked by their home office for guidelines on how to conduct the company during their absence. Here is a sample of some of the instructions they gave: "Stay within budget. . . . Don't hire MBAs. . . .Remember the customer is boss. . . .Get it in writing. . . .Don't do anything until I get back." There are umbrella values buried in these instructions. *What would your instructions be?*

When you are faced with difficult choices or decisions, what do you do? Think of some tough dilemmas you could be caught in such as product defects, quality and cost issues, potential cutbacks, hiring mistakes, and so on. Think through what you would choose to do in each case. Look at the umbrella values represented in your decision.

How do your organization's current umbrella values differ from its wished-for values? Go back through your answers to these questions about umbrella values and classify the values revealed in them as either "reality" or "wishes." If you are not sure about any one of them, put it under "wishes." If a value is current—visible in people's day-to-day work—you will know it without any doubt.

Compare the answers from several tribes about their values and look for potential warfare issues. Look at two or three different tribal definitions of quality and then develop two scenarios. In one scenario, picture the collision that could occur between these tribes because of their values differences. Tell yourself the story as it might occur: *What event would trigger the problem, and what would the tribes be likely to say to each other?* Now picture a second scenario. This time, imagine how these two or three tribes could blend their values to work as a team on producing some new innovation, or a service for a customer, or some internal operations improvement. *Which scenario sounds more like reality in your organization?*

Can you identify at least one symbol for each of the umbrella values you identified? This may be difficult to do at first. The symbols may be so obvious to you that you do not even consciously think of them anymore. Watch for symbols as you go about your work over the next few weeks.

Are these symbols based on a sincere commitment to the values they represent? Or are they window dressing, an attempt to cover up the fact that the practical effort to live out the value is not happening?

Who is your organization's "brand X"? Who is it the tribes can "love to hate"? An outside competitor can be the target for that fighting spirit among your tribes, which might otherwise compete with each other.

What are you proud of about your organization? People are rarely unable to answer this question. Your answer will reflect your tribal or umbrella values. If you choose to do so, you can use these values as a base for building an even stronger, values-driven organization.

5 TRIBAL TRAINING

When you start a new job in a company, you go through a great deal of training in the first few weeks. Some of this training is formal orientation in the company's policies and procedures, and some is instruction in the specific, technical content of the job. But other training is informal and occurs within your new tribe.

Tribes are usually very efficient at "training" their new members in appropriate tribal behavior. New employees must learn the tribe's behavior and language or face the possibility of never really being accepted by the group. It is a serious mistake for a new employee, at any level, to spend much time talking about "the way we did things at my old company." This is not welcome information to the new tribe. The best strategy is to listen and learn as much as possible, as quickly as possible. Later when the tribe has accepted you as a full-fledged member, it may be receptive to the "old" ideas, if they are carefully presented. But during the training and initiation phase, talk about the old company almost always triggers resentment.

This resentment even occurs at the top level in organizations. I have seen CEOs get themselves in trouble in a new organization by constantly referring to their old company during their first few months in a new company. Although no one says it directly to a CEO's face, I have often been told, "Why didn't he stay at the old company if it was so great?" Or, "He doesn't even know what's going on around here and he is already changing things. Why doesn't he at least visit our area first and see what we are doing?"

Differences in formal education and backgrounds have a significant impact on the ability of the various tribes to get along with each other. These differences are closely tied to the gaps in status, power, and income levels of the different tribes. A lawyer, a paralegal, and a secretary in a law firm have very different kinds of formal training, and no one has any doubt about the pecking order of these roles. In my experience, this is a very sensitive tribal characteristic.

FORMAL TRAINING

The education and training required of its members by each tribe is usually obvious. There is usually a general pattern of educational requirements that is more or less consistent within the tribe. Members of accounting tribes, nursing tribes, or sales tribes have usually gone through similar kinds of formal training, either through their education or through the training provided by the organization. Often previous training is a basic requirement for being offered the job in the first place; you cannot join the tribe if you are not educationally qualified. Education is often the only tribal characteristic that is actively used in the hiring process. Competence in the tribal language, thinking, values, and rules of the game, can be hard to measure in an interview, but training is easy to spot on a resume, often making it, in fact, overused as a screening device. If the other four characteristics could be identified as easily as educational background, they would probably be tested more often.

There are, of course, the exceptional people with unusual backgrounds who are asked to become members of a tribe, but often these people have a more difficult time gaining acceptance. For example, I know of one woman who is an assistant vice president of a financial division in a major corporation and who has no degree beyond high school. She accomplished this by sheer determination and talent, but her background is very unusual for both the finance and assistant vice president tribes. Especially as she entered the higher level management tribe, she was the target of an unusual amount of criticism about the way she reached that position and about her ability to handle it. Over time she proved her abilities and was finally accepted as a legitimate member of her new tribe, but it was a slower process for her than it would have been for someone with a more appropriate educational background.

This tribal characteristic is tied to the highly charged societal issues of socioeconomic background and class membership. Americans are famous for publicly pretending that these distinctions do not exist, or at least do not matter. "You do not talk about these things openly." But they do exist in our culture, and they do affect an individual's ability to enter certain tribes or to gain acceptance once they have joined them.

RITES OF PASSAGE

Rites of passage within a tribe are usually not as obvious as its formal training, although qualifying exams—such as CPA exams, law boards, Broker Series 7 exams, nursing state boards, and so on—are certainly one visible kind of initiation rite. But most rites of passage occur on the job and may be jokingly referred to by the tribe as "initiation" events. For instance:

- Surviving your first encounter with the famous "worst customer" when he arrives on his routine complaining spree: The new employee is sent into the fray, much to the amusement of all the other tribal members, who are behind the scenes watching the event. When the confrontation is over and the new employee returns to the group, he will usually be met with laughter, teasing, and backslapping. As an effective rite of passage, the harder a time the customer gave the new employee the better.

- Conquering a complicated skill for the first time: In any tribe there are complicated procedures or tasks that must be learned, such as processing a payroll run perfectly with no paychecks to cancel and write manually, or correctly installing a complicated piece of equipment. When a new employee masters one of these tasks, he has passed another rite of passage.

- Learning to use a particular piece of equipment: This is often especially important in tribes that use computers heavily. When the new member reaches the point of understanding how to use the equipment without having to ask constant questions, the other tribal members will see him as having arrived.

- Reaching a sales quota within a prescribed period of time: This is a classic rite of passage for new salespeople. Each sales tribe has its own standard for the level of sales that symbolizes successful entry into the tribe. Sometimes it will be the official quota that the company has set for the sales force, but it is not uncommon for the sales tribe to have its own standard, which may be higher than the official quota. You really have not arrived until you reach the tribe's own quota.

Rites of passage usually include the achievement of a certain skill level or productivity level, or surviving some unpleasant aspect of the job. Going through each rite of passage strengthens the new employee's bond with the other tribal members. This attachment increases the probability that once "fully inducted," he will staunchly defend his group against threats from other tribes.

STORYTELLING TRAINING

One of the most effective forms of tribal orientation is storytelling. For example, a new corporate employee goes to a formal orientation and is told that her primary responsibility is to respond to requests from the field office and to provide services. She then goes back to the department and is told by fellow tribal members that the real goal of the department is to produce as many billable hours as possible in the field. Her tribe proceeds to tell her stories about all the ways they find work—stretch out the projects, or billing for "customized" reports that are actually just duplicates from the word processor with a few name changes. Which training is the most believable to the new member—the formal orientation or the tribal stories? Within a week on a new job, most tribes have done a thorough and persuasive job of story telling training for a new tribal member.

A group of organizational culture researchers has categorized seven types of stories that occur frequently in most organizations. Each kind of story tells the employees as well as outsiders a great deal about the company and how it operates. The categories are described below, with examples from the research findings of both positive and negative stories.[1]

1. Breaking the Rules.   Companies have many stories about when to break the rules and when not to. These stories also instruct the tribes on the likely consequences of breaking rules. A positive story about breaking the rules is often that of a CEO being stopped by a front-line employee for trying to enter an area without satisfying the required safety precautions, or for violating some other restriction. The employee is rewarded with the CEO's praise for having the courage to enforce the rules even with top management.

At a major cosmetics company where there had been a problem with employees arriving late, a new receptionist was not so lucky. Everyone was required to sign in each morning. The head of the company, who was often late himself, one day stopped at the front desk to look over the list of sign-ins but was prevented from doing so by the new receptionist. She told him that no one was allowed to look at the list— she was under strict orders. The discussion went back and forth, with the receptionist being courteous but adamant that he was not allowed to look at the list. The CEO then asked her if she knew who he was. She replied that she did not. His response was, "Well, when you pick up your final paycheck this afternoon, ask 'em to tell ya."

These stories quickly spread a message to all tribes about how they are to behave. The message often includes the proviso that the rules only apply to people below a certain level in the organizational hierarchy.

2. Is the Boss Human?   These stories revolve around whether the status of the boss is more important than his human qualities. The status-versus-equality message is paramount in this kind of story. When there was a major strike at Illinois Bell back in the late 1960s, on weekends Charles Brown, the CEO,would pitch in to help repair phone lines. A call came in from his country club saying that they had a broken telephone and needed service. "Without batting an eye or changing clothes, Charlie [as he was known] went out and fixed the country club telephone." The people at Bell loved to tell that story and often teased him about it afterwards. By contrast, a senior officer at one of the large television networks would often walk onto the elevator, use his pass key, and make everyone else ride to his floor first because he did not want to wait.

3. Can the Little Person Rise to the Top?   That is, what is the response of the company to talented employees in low-status jobs? Are they rewarded with promotions and increased status? A clerk in a cashier's job caught the attention of Thomas Beck, the head of a division at Proctor and Gamble. Beck told the man that he was the first person he had ever seen who smiled as he paid out money. Beck remembered the man later and promoted him to a sales position. The clerk ended up as the general sales manager for the division.

4. Will I Get Fired?   These stories tell the tribes what to expect during hard times. Will we get laid off or not? How secure are our jobs? There are many stories about companies that cut back hours, but ask everyone to take a percentage pay cut, including the top officers during hard times. There also are many stories, however, that communicate a different message. At one company, a manager of a division was told in his first week of work to lay off forty people by the end of the day. When he asked about the procedure for doing this, the controller told him, "I don't care how you do it, but get rid of them. By the way, we quit here at 5:15 so don't notify anybody until 5:00. We want a full day's work out of them." The manager refused to do it, so the controller came to the department at 5:00 p.m., randomly picked forty people and notified them that they were dismissed.

5. Will the Organization Help Me When I Have to Move?   These stories are prevalent in companies that transfer their employees frequently, they tell employees how much help to expect from the company in their relocation. A 3M employee named Mai was in Vietnam with his family at the end of the Vietnam War. He and his family managed to get out of the country after many harrowing experiences and finally arrived in St. Paul with nothing but the clothes on their backs. Other 3M employees pitched in and took them shopping, housed them, tutored their children in English, and helped them settle into their new life in the United States.

6. How Will the Boss React to Mistakes?   Employees learn from these stories whether they will be routinely forgiven or punished for mistakes. One chairman was famous for being very unforgiving of anyone who lost an account. At each monthly meeting, he would recall some lost deal and publicly criticize the person responsible. He had a very long memory for these incidents and would bring them up repeatedly.

7. How Will the Organization Deal With Crisis?   This is the most common category of stories in organizations. The crisis can be external, such as weather, or internal, such as a technical problem. Any employee at whatever level can be the "star" of these stories. There is an AT&T story, which has been dubbed, "The Miracle on 14th Street," about a fire in

Manhattan that wiped out the telephone system in one entire area of the city. AT&T mobilized the largest response team it has ever had. At one point they had 4,000 employees working around the clock to restore service. The theme of taking control, or the inability to do so, is present in these crisis stories.

People love to tell stories, and they also want to hear them. They use these kinds of stories as blueprints for their own behavior when faced with similar situations. The stories may often be exaggerated or even totally fabricated, but usually the theme or point of the story is accurate. Some stories are told throughout an organization, while others are told within specific tribes that are giving new members information about how to deal with the rest of the organization. Without story telling training, it would be much more difficult for an employee to learn the ropes of a new organization and to become a loyal tribal member.

TRIBAL LOYALTY

One of the main purposes of all forms of training within an organization is to increase the employees' clan loyalty—either to the organization or to their tribes. Tribal training, however, can have an us-versus-them quality. It has advantages and disadvantages for the organization. The main disadvantage is that high levels of tribal loyalty are likely to trigger more tribal warfare. When a person is extremely loyal to his own tribe, he is more likely to see his tribe's perspective as the only right answer. The advantage of tribal loyalty, however, is having strong teams that pull together well and do not waste as much time and energy on conflicts within the tribe. High quality and peak performance from a tribe require a tight team and a minimum of fighting.

As I stated at the beginning of this book, my advice is to be careful about trying to change the tribes and their characteristics. Tribal loyalty is valuable not only to the organization but to the mental health of employees. What I do advise is teaching these tight teams to communicate with each other, being careful not to threaten their sense of loyalty.

QUESTIONS TO ASK ABOUT TRIBAL TRAINING
IN YOUR COMPANY

What is the typical educational background of members of your own tribe? List several other tribes and describe the educational background that is typical in those groups. If there are wide gaps in educational background between the tribes, there is more likelihood for conflict. Sometimes these differences represent an unspoken class system within the organization. Everyone knows which tribes have the most status and the best financial rewards. They also know that you cannot enter those tribes without a certain educational background. Ask yourself if your company gives real support to employees who want to get the education it takes to break into new tribes. Or do they have to leave your company to do that? For example, some companies have the informal rule, "Once a secretary, always a secretary." If a secretary gets more education, it is still very difficult to break the barrier to entering any other position.

What are the rites of passage in your tribe? When has a new member "arrived" or been initiated? Rites of passage usually involve (1) achieving a certain skill level, (2) achieving a specified productivity level, or (3) surviving some unpleasant aspect of the job. What were your specific rites of passage when you were new in your tribe?

Think of two or three stories you have heard in the past month within your tribe. *If a new tribal member heard these stories, what "training" would he receive?* Who are the good guys in the stories, and who is the enemy? Ask yourself whether you would ever be likely to hear the same story in another tribe in the organization. If you would hear it everywhere in the company, then it is likely to be an organizationwide story with a message for everyone who works there. If, on the other hand, it is a story that would only be told in your own tribe and no place else, then it is likely to offer training to your tribal members only.

Look back at the categories of stories that are common in organizations ("Breaking the Rules," "Is the Boss Human?" and so on). See if you can think of at least one story from your own organization that fits in each category. You may not be able to come up with a story for all of them, but you will probably be able to cover most of them. *Do you have positive or negative stories?* What is the moral of each story? If you were a new employee, what would each story tell you about how to behave in this organization?

Look over your answers to the questions above and think back to your own training when you were a new tribal member. How long did it take your tribe to train you? *What would have happened if you had been untrainable or had refused to develop any loyalty to the tribe?*

What kind of training does your organization provide to bring the tribes together to learn about each other and to negotiate the differences between them? Do people from different areas of your company even know each other's names or job functions? If you plan to get these groups together to discuss interfunctional work, try to include as many levels as you can. It is, of course, helpful to get only the managers together, but all the members of the tribes need the education. Be sure that the focus of your training is on the connections between the tribes. Look for improvements, not for blame.

6 TRIBAL THINKING PATTERNS

People usually assume that thinking is an automatic process that cannot be controlled. Like being on "automatic pilot" it just happens somewhere in the brain. Most people do have habitual thinking patterns that they have used most of their lives, not knowing where these patterns came from or how they were learned. There are logical thinkers, methodical thinkers, spacey thinkers, emotional thinkers and so on. Obviously these different ways of thinking can be confusing or irritating when two people are trying to communicate with each other.

Ned Herrmann, a researcher in the area of thinking and brain functioning gives us a good example of how a person's thinking affects the way he goes about performing a task or job.[1] Imagine that you have purchased an unassembled bicycle for a child for Christmas. It is Christmas Eve, and you are down to the wire—you have to get the thing put together and placed under the tree before the next morning. You could accomplish this particular task, using one of two approaches, which represent very different patterns of thinking. As you read about each approach, decide for yourself which one sounds like the way you would put the bicycle together. If you are married or ever have been, it can be interesting to also think about how your spouse would put together the bicycle. If the two of you would take opposite approaches to this task, then you match the statistical average for married couples. When it comes to thinking, opposites truly do attract.

The first assembler would begin by organizing the parts. He would probably place all the large parts in one pile, the medium-sized parts in a second pile, and the small parts in a third. Next, he would get out the nuts and bolts and separate them into separate piles by size and shape. Then he would get out the instruction sheet and begin the dreaded task of trying to decipher what is supposed to be done. All instruction sheets are very annoying, but he will do the best he can in making sense of the step-by-step instructions and diagrams. He will study step one, put the relevant parts together, then go on to step two, step three and so forth. At the end there will, of course, be two parts left over. It always happens. So he will go back through the instructions and hunt for a clue as to where the two parts fit, taking apart the bicycle as he goes to be ready to add them in the proper places.

The second kind of thinker will rip open the end of the box, and dump the parts out on the floor. He will then spread them all out so that one is not on top of the other. Now comes a very important step. He will get up off the floor and walk a few steps away to get a "bird's-eye view" of all the parts. The instruction sheet is stuck down in the bottom of the box, never to be given another thought. "That thing is a piece of garbage and no help at all!" But there is a photograph of the bicycle on the outside of the box—now that's helpful. He will study the picture and look at the parts for a few minutes, then dive in, piecing parts together and taking them apart over and over again until everything fits and the bicycle works. There are, of course, two parts left over, just as in the first approach. That fact never changes. But this assembler's reaction to the two leftover parts is dramatically different. He picks them up and deposits them in the nearest trash can! "The thing works—what else do you want?" In the meantime, the first assembler is still hunting for where those two parts fit.

The differences between the two approaches are obvious. Now think about these two kinds of people trying to work together. Imagine one of those opposite-thinking married couples assembling the bicycle together on Christmas Eve. Theory would suggest that the two of them should make the best possible toy assembly team, that they would bring the full range of thinking skills to bear on the task. But anyone who has ever lived with someone who thinks in a different way knows that if those two people try to work as a team on that bicycle on Christmas Eve, they probably will not be speaking to each other by Christmas morning. The difference in the way each approaches the task is very irritating to the other. And besides, they are both convinced that their own approach is right. Think about it from the point of view of the person who is trying to follow the instructions. He's studying step three, he has it just about figured out, and he looks up to find his partner cramming parts together that are not even mentioned until step five in the instructions! Unless they both have the patience of Job, argument is inevitable.

EXPLANATIONS FOR WHY PEOPLE THINK DIFFERENTLY

Some researchers believe that thinking differences actually have a physiological basis in separate parts of the brain. Others say that these differences are more personality-based. The reasons for the distinct patterns of mental functioning are difficult to test, so there is a great deal of controversy among researchers about the physiological or psychological basis of observed thinking differences. From a practical point of view, however, the reasons why these patterns occur is less important than the fact that hundreds of thousands of surveys confirm that the patterns do exist.

In the bicycle story, the first person is a logical, factual, linear thinker, and the second person is a visual, spatial, intuitive thinker—left hemisphere-thinking and right-hemisphere thinking, respectively. The left hemisphere is where the language center is located in most people's brains. Many researchers believe that this is the reason that logical, linear thought processes are more specialized in the left hemisphere. The right hemisphere is the silent side of the brain for the most part, and it appears to have a more highly developed capacity for visual and spatial thinking. Although people, of course, blend the two patterns together all the time in their thinking, most of us have a clear-cut tendency toward one or the other. It is not known at this point whether those tendencies are psychologically, physiologically, genetically, or environmentally learned. But there is common agreement that the two distinct patterns of thinking and behaving do exist.

Ned Herrmann divides thinking into four patterns.[2] Using a survey that he has developed, it is possible to establish an individual's preference for one or more of the four patterns. Everyone uses all four, but most people have a clear preference for one or two, as well as one mode of thinking that is clearly their least preferred. Other researchers in the field of Jungian psychology produce similar results using a survey called the Myers Briggs Type Indicator.[3] (Other surveys also produce similar

Figure 6–1. The Four Thinking Patterns Revisited

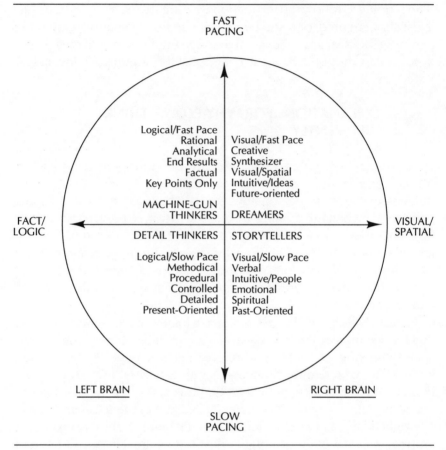

Source: Adapted from Ned Herrmann, "The Creative Brain," *Training and Development Journal* (October 1981); and Isabel B. Myers and Peter B. Myers, *Gifts Differing* (Palo Alto, Cal.: Consulting Psychological Press, 1980).

results, but these are the two that correlate most closely and have the most substantial research behind them.)

These four patterns have important implications for tribal communication because there are usually consistent, predictable thinking preferences exhibited by different tribes. No one has to tell you that a lawyer, an artistic designer, and a social worker do not usually think in the same gear. Within your organization similar tribal patterns of thinking are likely to exist. Figure 6–2 lists a few occupational tribes in the quadrant representing their dominant thinking preference.

Figure 6–2.   Who Think How

MACHINE-GUN THINKERS			DREAMERS
	Lawyers Physicians Chief Financial Officers School superintendents Scientists	Architects Artists Entrepreneurs Marketing/Advertising Strategic planners	
DETAIL THINKERS	Quality control Engineers Manufacturing foremen Middle managers Accountants	Social workers Personnel Nurses Homemakers Teachers	STORYTELLERS

Source: These descriptions are derived from Ned Herrmann, Scoring Notebook and Isabel Briggs Myers, *Manual: Guide to Development and use of the Myers Briggs Type Indicator* (Palo Alto, Cal.: Consulting Psychologists Press, 1986), p. 244.

THE FOUR PATTERNS OF THINKING:

As you read about the four thinking patterns, think about your own preference and try to rank the patterns, from the one you most prefer down to the one you least prefer. Chances are that you have the most difficulty communicating with individuals or tribes that rely heavily on your least preferred mode of thinking. You can do it, but it takes more energy.

People often say that it feels like swimming against the current to think and communicate in a pattern that they do not like. But many times a person's thinking preference does not match his thinking skill. He may have become quite skillful in a particular kind of thinking, even though he does not actually like it very much. Many people tell me that this is true of the thinking they do at work. They tell me that they use a great deal of logical, factual, linear thinking at work, with a great deal of skill, but actually prefer visual, spatial, intuitive thinking in their personal life.

I work with one corporate division head who is known as a hard-driving, detail-oriented, factual thinker. But it is clear in talking with him on nonwork topics that he is a great storyteller, visualizer, and dreamer. I have kidded him with the accusation that he is a "closet right-brainer." In talking with his staff, he has now begun to use more of his ability in intuitive, visual thinking. The change has come as a great surprise to many of the people who have known him in the work setting for a long time, and as a relief to the right-brain thinkers in his division.

Machine-gun Thinker

What I call the "machine-gun" thinker is a very fast-paced, logical thinker who fires factual and concise questions and comments. They want you to give them short precise answers—just the facts. . . .just the facts. One of their mottoes in life is, "Would you get to the point!" They do not want you to tell them the whole story from beginning to end. They want you to pick out the two or three most important facts, deliver them, and then be quiet. They can take any subject and summarize it into a few key items. These people are often very skillful at the "clean-up" thinking in an organization—critiquing, honing down, targeting a group's efforts.

If your goal in life was to drive machine-gun thinkers crazy, there are some very simple communication techniques that you could use to do it. Simply respond to one of their rapid-fire questions by telling them a story! Make it a very long story, and stop several times during the story to digress. Tell them the life history of every character in the story, and add several sideline stories as you go along. By the end of your long-winded story, make sure that you have forgotten the point of it and how it related to what the machine-gun thinker asked you in the first place. His blood pressure will be up, and he will probably start yelling at you somewhere in the middle of this story about getting to the point.

Now, of course, if you are not trying to harass a machine-gun thinker, you would use the opposite technique—getting to the point quickly, telling them only the end of the story, and sticking to two or three key facts about the topic. If you send a machine-gun thinker a memo, make sure it is no longer than one page, and put the key points in bulleted items so that the point of the memo is obvious at a glance. If you send a six-page memo and do not get to the point until the fifth page, a machine-gun thinker is likely to end up wondering about your mental capacities.

A machine-gun thinker who is the head of a sales company described his frustration with weekly meetings in his office that were intended to be one-hour overviews of projects in progress. He always wants to get through the list quickly—hitting the key points only—and be finished with the discussion in one hour or less. Several of the other members of the team want to stop at each item and discuss implementation details; they want his exact thinking on specific aspects of each project. It is a wrestling match every week over which kind of thinking wins.

Detail Thinker

This kind of thinking is also factual and logical, but a detail thinker uses facts in a way very different from that of the machine-gun thinker. The detail thinkers are interested in *all* the facts and will usually give them to you in a sequential or chronological order. They are slower paced than the machine-gun thinkers—not slower, of course, in intelligence, but slower because they are processing more detail and it simply takes more time. These people are usually more concerned about the detailed accuracy of what they are saying or doing than they are about racing through at top speed. Because they handle details well, they are usually very good implementers and will follow through on projects in a reliable and accurate way.

The detail thinkers have memories like a steel trap for factual detail. If a detail thinker asks you a question, he wants you to be sure that your answer is factually accurate. If you do not know the answer, he wants you to say so and then to go find out the right answer. Guessing is a dangerous strategy to use with a detail thinker. Salespeople often get themselves in trouble with detail-thinking clients; if you guess wrong, with clients, they will remember your mistake forever! And it will be very difficult to ever regain their trust, especially if that kind of mistake happens more than once.

When you listen to a detail thinker talk, it often sounds like an agenda of information. He may actually be ticking off the step-by-step points on his fingers as each point is covered. He will be procedural in his explanations and will give you the detailed steps he wants you to follow to get the job done. In contrast, a machine-gun thinker is much more likely to tell you only the end result he wants, expecting you to fill in the details yourself.

Individuals or tribes of people who use these two kinds of thinking often find each other quite annoying. The pacing difference alone causes problems. In addition, detail thinkers often say that the machine-gun thinkers are arrogant and rude. At the same time, however, the machine-gun thinkers are quick to tell you that the detail thinkers are tedious, boring, and probably not too smart anyway.

Dreamers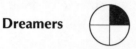

This form of thinking is more visual, spatial, and intuitive than logical and factual. Dreamers think in concepts, images, and ideas. They are the thinkers most likely to be attracted to risk and change. Dreamers are skillful at generating new ideas, alternatives, and visions of the future often talk in metaphors and analogies. Their thinking and talking is usually "thematic"; moreover, they will switch themes or topics in midsentence and go off in any other direction that catches their attention. In organizations they are skillful in the start-up roles (not in follow-through) and in the creative, intuitive functions.

Dreamer thinking is often referred to as the "entrepreneurial quadrant" because people who start their own businesses almost always receive high scores in this category on the surveys used to measure thinking preferences. Entrepreneurs, like most people, usually have high scores in several quadrants, but consistently score highest in dreamer thinking. If a person scores high in this quadrant and low in the other three on Herrmann's survey, he calls this pattern the "entrepreneurially bankrupt" profile.[4] Without some left-brain thinking to back up the dreamer approach, this kind of business owner is likely to move on to new products and ideas faster than any of them can be brought to market and profit. The data from the surveys indicate that entrepreneurs who have gone bankrupt often have a strong preference for dreamer thinking and very little inclination for the other kinds of thinking.

Dreamer thinking is very fast-paced, in some ways even faster than machine-gun thinking. The direction of this thinking is toward the future and toward new ideas, and its momentum does not necessarily allow stopping to examine the facts. Often when a person or tribe is called "flaky," someone who is a logical, linear thinker is describing dreamer thinking. Dreamer thinkers are often "in a fog," not thinking in any orderly way about the details around them. These people tell us that they go to run errands and come back with everything *except* what was on the list. Or they call to ask for a wake-up call in a hotel and when the operator asks for their room number, they read out the area code on the telephone. One person told me about pulling up to a fast-food restaurant, drive-through line, ordering a sandwich, paying for it, and then driving off without the food. And so on. This kind of thinking is utterly mysterious to a logical, factual thinker.

Storytellers

Storytellers are also intuitive and visual, but they have a more detailed focus on feelings and people. "Gut feel" is a term that many people use to describe the way this kind of thinker just "knows" how someone is feeling or what is going on below the surface between two people. The more extroverted of these thinkers love to meet new people every-where they go and are often entertaining storytellers. Their stories are usually filled with characters, but may not have any particular point beyond the entertainment value and pleasure of telling them. "Would you get to the point?" is a meaningless and irritating interruption to them. In organizations they are often skillful at handling morale and human relations issues. "What about the people?" is one of their mottoes.

Storytellers emphasize teamwork, relationships, and participation. They often have the most difficulty communicating effectively with logical, bottom-line thinkers, (the machine-gun thinkers). They are likely to criticize others for having no feelings, and they are often accused of being the company's "bleeding hearts." If these people are cast in diplomat or facilitator roles in an organization, they will often be very skillful at pulling warring factions together—at getting them to see each other's point of view. But often storytellers are as caught up in the conflicts as everyone else. They are looking at the issues from the per-spective of concern for morale, trust, and teamwork and can be quick to conclude that others are insensitive or uncaring.

THINKING CLASHES BETWEEN THE TRIBES

Within each tribe in the organization there are usually one or two of these thinking modes that are considered the "right" way to think. Finance, engineering, purchasing, business office, and most of the specialist or technical tribes tend to favor logical, factual, left-brain approaches. Sales, marketing, research, design, personnel, customer service, public relations, communications, or other generalist tribes often tend toward the right-brain thinking of the dreamers or story-tellers.

Even if the thinking pattern of an individual within one of these tribes does not match the tribal thinking pattern, that individual will tend to behave at work in the way that fits the tribe. When your personal and tribal thinking patterns do not match, you usually feel more stress and will burn out more easily. It takes more energy to work in a job that requires you to think in away different from what comes naturally for you. Some of the extreme career shifts that people make in mid-life can be traced back to the fact that the thinking required in their old jobs did not match their personal preference. Finally, they had enough of it and decided to shift into a career that was a better fit for them.

Many of the conflicts that occur between generalist and specialist tribes are partly due to their thinking differences.

- The detail-thinking specialist answers the storytelling generalist's question, "Can I do it?" by pulling out a regulatory letter and reading it all from beginning to end.

- The detail-thinking specialist wants the forms filled out correctly by a dreamer-thinking generalist, who is focused on the future and new directions.

- The machine-gun thinking specialist in research analysis tries to tell the storytelling generalist from Marketing the key facts needed to accurately represent the product to the customer. The story-teller does not listen well enough to remember any of these important facts.

Some tribal or individual conflicts do not relate to the different functions of the generalist and the specialist. They are strictly collisions in thinking.

- The machine-gun thinker asks the detail thinker, "What happened at the meeting I missed?" He wants a one-sentence answer that gives him the end results, the decisions made at the meeting. The detail thinker responds by giving a detailed account of the entire agenda for the meeting.

- The machine-gun–thinking chief financial officer is focused on revenue problems and is pushing for layoffs. The story telling human-resources director is concerned about the impact of layoffs on morale and customer services.

- The dreamer R&D technician is trying to "inspire" a detail thinker with his latest idea. The detail thinker responds with, "What's wrong with the way we are doing it now? And if we are going to make the change, what is your implementation plan?"

These battles fall into predictable patterns based on which kind of thinking each combatant is using. The following themes are often the underlying issues causing the conflict.

Facts	versus	Ideas
Fast-paced	versus	Slow-paced
Details	versus	Big Picture
Practicality	versus	Fantasy
Logic	versus	Feelings

When I listen to the two sides presenting their points of view in these conflicts, I sometimes find that they are not as far apart on the content of what each is saying as it seems. It is the way each of them says it that is irritating and confusing to the other. Being forced to listen to stories when all you want are the key facts puts the machine-gun thinker in the mood to argue. Being told, "Get to the point!" one too many times does not leave the storyteller in a negotiable frame of mind. Having to listen to the wild-eyed fantasies of the dreamers is a total waste of time to a detail thinker. On the other hand, being grilled about implementation details will leave the dreamer feeling as though he is being "pecked to death by baby ducks." The process of communicating with someone who thinks very differently is exhausting. And after all that frustration, you may end up discovering that you were all saying basically the same thing in the first place.

Everyone has the capacity to think and communicate in all four patterns. But because most people think automatically in only one or two, learning to communicate with different kinds of thinkers requires developing the flexibility to switch gears. When you and another person communicate in two different patterns, each of you has to translate what the other is saying into your own language. This takes energy and can be irritating. There is also a significant chance that the translation will be inaccurate and will cause misunderstanding. A few days later, one of you hears the other one repeating what he thought was said. And it is not what you said at all! The natural conclusion at this point is that the

Figure 6–3.   Ways to Communicate With Each Type of Thinker.

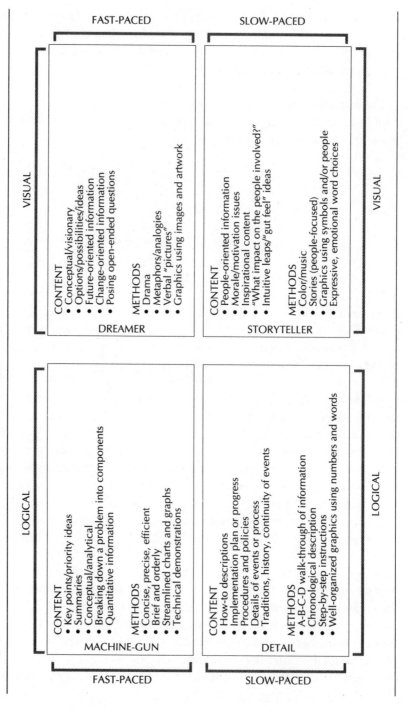

FAST-PACED   SLOW-PACED

VISUAL

DREAMER

CONTENT
• Conceptual/visionary
• Options/possibilities/ideas
• Future-oriented information
• Change-oriented information
• Posing open-ended questions

METHODS
• Drama
• Metaphors/analogies
• Verbal "pictures"
• Graphics using images and artwork

STORYTELLER

CONTENT
• People-oriented information
• Morale/motivation issues
• Inspirational content
• "What impact on the people involved?"
• Intuitive leaps/"gut feel" ideas

METHODS
• Color/music
• Stories (people-focused)
• Graphics using symbols and/or people
• Expressive, emotional word choices

VISUAL

LOGICAL

MACHINE-GUN

CONTENT
• Key points/priority ideas
• Summaries
• Conceptual/analytical
• Breaking down a problem into components
• Quantitative information

METHODS
• Concise, precise, efficient
• Brief and orderly
• Streamlined charts and graphs
• Technical demonstrations

DETAIL

CONTENT
• How-to descriptions
• Implementation plan or progress
• Procedures and policies
• Details of events or process
• Traditions, history, continuity of events

METHODS
• A-B-C-D walk-through of information
• Chronological description
• Step-by-step instructions
• Well-organized graphics using numbers and words

LOGICAL

FAST-PACED   SLOW-PACED

other person either did not listen to what you said or is lying and purposely misrepresenting your comments. Either conclusion leads to trouble. Chances are, however, that neither assumption is correct. The other person probably did listen, but then translated the message into his own language and changed your original meaning without even realizing it.

The best solution to this problem is to present your own translation. If you are a storyteller talking to a machine-gun thinker, do not tell him a story—not unless you are purposely trying to run his blood pressure up! Before you walk into the machine-gun thinker's office, pick out two to four key facts, then go in and relate them, keeping your delivery concise and staccato. Then comes the hardest step of all for a story teller. Once you have fired your facts at the machine-gun thinker, stop talking!

The machine-gun thinker can learn to tell a story or give an example to explain a point. It will feel uncomfortable at first, but just like any new skill, it gets easier with practice. Dreamers can make detailed lists or lay out charts to help them communicate more effectively with detail thinkers. And detail thinkers can stop for a few minutes to picture the future, before getting back to the details of making the present happen. Figure 6–3 contains a few suggestions on how to communicate with a tribe or an individual with a thinking pattern different from yours. These are ways to switch gears and control the "translation" from your language to theirs.

PACING DIFFERENCES

Pacing differences in thought processes are another common source of conflict. Learning to speed up or slow down your pacing to match that of the person you are trying to communicate with is an important element of successful communication. Research in linguistics has determined that when two people are communicating effectively, they unconsciously fall into a synchronized rhythm and pacing of their movements.[5] Apparently this rhythm cannot be faked. If you are not really listening, the synchronizing will not occur. Most adults will experience this lack of synchronization as an irritation or as an uncomfortable sensation. A child feeling out of sync, however, will often confront you right away: "Hey, you're not listening to me!"

Pacing is a communication pattern that causes everyone a great deal of stress. Most people are so used to their own pace that they find it difficult to adjust to someone who is talking at a faster or slower pace. Fast-paced thinkers often get impatient, interrupt frequently, and try to rush the other person. People who are slower in their thinking often feel that they are racing to keep up, are being rushed, or are not being listened to. Both experiences are frustrating and produce stress. Since there is no way to avoid contact with many people using a wide range of pacing, the only way to protect your own stress level and to communicate effectively is to develop the ability to change pace. If you are trying to slow down, focus on details, both factual and personal. If you are trying to speed up, focus on summaries and overviews and stick to only a few facts or ideas. It takes practice, but people can learn to speed up or slow down.

QUESTIONS TO ASK ABOUT YOUR TRIBES' THINKING PATTERNS

In the diagnostic below, a few questions taken primarily from Ned Herrmann's survey form will give you an indication of your own thinking preferences.[6] You can also apply this test to each of your organization's tribes and decide how each one might answer these questions.

Which words best describe the way you think?

Machine-gun	*Dreamer*
Analytical	Conceptual
Logical	Creative
Rational	Intuitive (about solutions)
Critical	Innovative
Quantitative	Synthesizing
Factual	Simultaneous
Problem-solving	Spatial
Technical	Change-oriented

Detail	*Storyteller*
Controlled	Intuitive (about people)
Detailed	Communicative
Organized	Expressive
Planning-oriented	Verbal
Sequential	Spiritual
Reliable	Symbolic

Administrative	Emotional
Implementation-oriented	Musical

Rank your thinking preferences. Which of these four patterns do you like the most, not so much, even less, and least of all?
Now think about your skill level in each area, as opposed to your preference. *Are you skillful in some modes of thinking that you do not like?* Skill and preference often correlate, but sometimes you can be very skillful in a kind of thinking that you do not like.
List several of the tribes in your organization. *What do you think are each tribe's most preferred and least preferred modes of thinking?*
Pick two of the tribes that have very different thinking preferences. *What kinds of conflicts occur between these two groups?* Think of several specific examples. Analyze the conflict, and decide if any aspect of the difficulty between them is attributable to thinking differences.
Look over the following themes which are key elements in the different ways people think. Decide which word in each pair of words describes your own tribe most accurately. *How flexible are your tribal members in switching themes?*

Facts	versus	Ideas
Fast pacing	versus	Slow pacing
Details	versus	Big picture
Practicality	versus	Fantasy
Logic	versus	Feelings

Think about the pacing in your tribe. *How much do pacing differences cause you problems?* Does your tribe irritate you? Do you irritate any of its members? Do you interrupt frequently or get interrupted frequently? Interruptions are the best cue that the pacing between two people is not meshing. When you notice the interruptions, try speeding up or slowing down your own pace and see what happens. Even if you are not interested in the effect of pacing on communication, you may want to consider its role in stress. Fighting everyone else's pacing is a very stressful activity. You will never win, but you can wear yourself out trying.

7 TRIBAL RULES OF THE GAME

The rules of the game are the strategies or tactics used by a tribe to get the job done. Methods, actions, tricks of the trade, ploys—all can be rules of the game. They often operate as, mottoes for a tribe, as phrases or advice that is repeated over and over among the tribal members. It is a rare occasion when anyone within the tribe dares to question one of these rules. But such questions or challenges usually do not occur to a well-trained tribal member. The rules are so obviously right that there is nothing to discuss or challenge. If all those other people outside the tribe could only understand how important these things are, then everything would be fine.

During a seminar on identifying tribes, the truckers' tribe proudly announced to the group that their number one rule was: "Get the damn thing off the truck no matter what condition it is in, and get on to the next delivery." There had been a lot of laughing over in their corner as they were coming up with their rules, and they were all grinning from ear to ear when their spokesman presented this rule. The distribution, service, and sales tribes all groaned and shook their heads as they heard it. Agreeing that it was one of the truckers' tribal rules, everyone did manage to laugh. But it was clear which tribe was enjoying itself the most at that point.

In one company that I worked with, "Headquarters doesn't understand" was a private motto of the management tribe in a field division office. That rule carries many subrules: "Don't tell them unless they ask," "Only good news goes to Corporate," "Don't ask permission—apologize later if necessary." If a member of this management tribe questions those rules or behaves in a way that violates them, the tribe reacts strongly. Anger, reprimand, or tribal "shunning" would be a likely response to a member who told too much to corporate headquarters. In fact, the tribal members told me in confidence that one "talkative" member who did break the rules was "not too smart," and "a first-class fool."

RULES AND VALUES:
TWO SIDES OF THE SAME COIN

Rules of the game and tribal values are very closely linked. It is very unlikely that you will have one without the other. If values are the beliefs or the reasons for *what* the tribes do within the organization (for example, staying close to the customer), the rules tell the tribal members *how* to accomplish that value ("Always return your phone calls," "Never lie to the customer," "If you don't know the answer, say so and find out quickly"). Contrast "Stay close to the customer" with "High commissions at all costs." The rules of the game will be quite different in these cases. With the latter value, rules may be, "Only return the phone calls of the big clients," "Lie to the customer only if it is necessary to make the sale," and, "Tell the customer what he wants to hear whether you are sure or not!"

A tribe or organization may eloquently describe its values related to customers, quality, employee relations, and so forth. If, however, the rules you see them working by contradict these values statements, the tribe is lying to you, or to itself. When you see this contradiction, believe the rules and behaviors, not the stated values. It may be that the stated value is a "wished-for" value—something that the tribe wants to be proud of and to work towards, but which they have not made a reality. Pretending these values are real is dangerous to the organization. Everyone knows at some level that such values are not real, and most will resent the pretense. Cynicism is an inevitable outcome of a values-rules gap, along with confusion, ethical dilemmas for employees, and lower productivity.

THE POWER OF TRIBAL RULES

Rules of the game are a very powerful and stable tribal characteristic. They evolve over time and are considered the justifiable means to reach the desired end. These rules are learned on the job as a part of the informal training from the veteran tribal members, and they are learned quickly—usually within a few days. Failing to learn and follow the informal tribal rules of the game will brand a new member as an outsider, or even mark him or her as the enemy. For example, everyone has heard stories of assembly-line workers' reactions to a new employee who works at a speed much faster than the established pattern. The new employee is rarely successful at changing the existing tribal rule—or even at lasting very long in the job—if he is unable to adapt.

Tribal rules help to shed some light on why corporate strategic plans often fail. An organization's strategic plan is usually developed by the board of directors and top-management personnel. They are focused on the future and on the big picture for the company. They may even have done a very good job of building enough flexibility into the plan so that the company can adapt as market conditions change. The planning meeting is adjourned, and everyone is satisfied. But the question that no one asked is: In what ways does this strategic plan affect the day-to-day behavior and rules of the various tribes in the organization?

If the strategic plan requires a number of behaviors to change in many tribes throughout the organization, it will fail unless something is done to manage and promote the rules and behavior changes. The tribal rules must eventually match the new plan. Usually the tribes do not argue with management about the new plan—they simply do nothing new. This may be an intentional effort to sabotage the new plan. (NIH stands for "Not Invented Here" and is a common rule for many tribes.) If the tribes were not involved in developing the plan, they may not care if it succeeds or not, and in fact, sometimes they may actually want the plan to fail. In many cases, however, the tribes are not intentionally trying to sabotage the company's new strategic plan. It simply does not occur to them that a number of their rules and daily behaviors need to change to make the plan work. If the tribes are busy and under a lot of pressure, they are not likely to stop to analyze their rule in light of the new strategic plan. Besides, many of their rules are so much a part of their routines that tribes are often not even aware of their existence, making them unaware that alternative rules and behaviors might work as well or even better.

EXAMPLES OF TRIBAL RULES

There are hundreds of tribal rules in every organization. Many of them are unique to a particular company, but some common themes show up over and over again. To help you get started in your thinking about your organization's tribal rules, a number of common examples are described below. The examples or rules are clustered under the tribal values that they relate to. A number of the rules are connected to more than one value , so placing a rule under just one value is not always accurate. Nevertheless, the arrangement below should help to organize your thinking about your organization's rules and the beliefs that they are based on. These examples represent the common statements, or mottoes that I have heard when listening to tribes describe themselves and the way they work.

Value

Staying close to customer	Caring more about what customers buy than what they think

Rules

"The customer is always right."	"The customer is a noisy nuisance."
"Don't be afraid to say, 'I don't know,' then get back to them with the right answer."	"Never say, 'I don't know.'"
"Always return phone calls."	"Only return phone calls from good customers" (meaning, big buyers).
"Never screen my calls—I want my customers to know I'm available."	"Screen all my calls so I don't have to answer when it's an angry customer."
"I guarantee my services—I will fix it or refund it."	"Once it's sold, my job is done."

These examples are just the tip of the iceberg on customer rules. If you sit and listen to a sales tribe or public relations tribe talk about their customers, the mottoes and rules will come up in almost every sentence. When they complain about "problem customers," they are describing the people who push them to break their rules. For example, in the brokerage industry one of the rules for brokers is, "Sell fast and keep moving." The least favorite kind of customer for most brokers is the one who wants to be sent the prospectus then calls with twelve detailed questions that require research to answer. After he thinks it over for several days, he decides to look at two or three other product options, and then finally buys. These customers make many brokers apoplectic before the sale is closed.

Value

Innovation—dreaming up new ideas that convert into practical products and operations improvements	Traditionalism—protection of the status quo and the "way we've always done things here"

Rules

"Advertise your failures within the company to see if anybody can use the idea for something else."	"Bury any failure."
"Don't ask permission, apologize later if necessary."	"If you don't have permission, don't do it."
"Flexibility is the key—be ready to change course at any point."	"Rules are rules."
"Why are we still doing it that way?"	"Why should we change it?"
"Stay quiet about your new idea until it is too late to stop it."	"Pay attention to the bottom line" (this year's bottom line!).
"Planning is a loose process that changes constantly."	"Planning is a clear-cut process that determines budgets and strict guidelines for the next year."

Interactions between innovative and traditionalist tribes are among the most common sources of tribal warfare in organizations. Innovators will tell you that the traditionalists are boring and lay awake nights thinking of ways to be the company's official "wet blanket." Innovative tribes will often tell you that they are willing to lie to the traditionalist tribes whenever necessary. It is the only way to get anything new done. In his book about internal innovators in organizations, *Intrapreneuring*, Gifford Pinchot says that an organization has an immune system much like the human body. When a company senses a new idea afoot, the idea is surrounded and killed as quickly as possible. His advice is to keep a low profile on new ideas until they are well developed.[1]

The traditionalist tribes, of course, have their side of the story as well. They give anyone who will listen the heartfelt advice to never let those other tribes get control of a budget! They use words like *wild-eyed* or *irresponsible* to describe the innovators. They will often admit that the company needs those tribes, which must nevertheless be kept under control.

Value

Employee Involvement— taking care of the employees and involving them in decisions so that they will take care of the company	Productivity—maximizing the efficient use of all resources, including human resources, regardless of the personal consequences

Rules

"'High touch' as well as high tech is important here."	"We operate like a family here."
"We have a no-layoff policy."	"Layoffs are necessary tools for controlling market swings."
"The people closest to the action have the best ideas for solving problems."	"Experts are most likely to come up with efficient solutions to problems."
"If it takes more time to involve employees in change, it is worth the expense in the long run."	"Competition is what motivates people—interteam rivalry is good for the company."
"Teamwork is the way to get things done."	"Keep it simple—streamlining and moving fast are more important than getting everyone's opinion."

"Some things cannot be measured, such as the value of employee morale."

"If you can't measure it, it does not exist, or at least isn't useful."

"We need to trust our employees and work with them to improve their performance."

"We have got to follow the legal guidelines and carefully document any employee problems."

Many tribes are a mixture of these of values and rules about employees and productivity; that is, many attempt the difficult balancing act of combining the best of these values and rules in a way that is both humane and efficient. There are, however, many tribes and organizations that lean heavily toward one value or the other. Or perhaps an organization sends out a mixed message: the official values are people-oriented, but organizational behavior indicates to the employees that they are cogs in the wheel and of very little importance. Low morale and employee hostility are the usual results. Employees fare better in an organization that is openly productivity-oriented and takes a fairly hard-nosed approach to human-resources issues. At least the message is consistent, and employees can feel that they know where they stand.

One woman discussed with me her dilemma about working overtime. I had been "warned" that she was uncooperative, unable to keep up with her work, and unwilling to do what it took to catch up and stay caught up. In fact, her job was in jeopardy. Her side of the story, however, sounded very different. She said she worked long overtime hours and was "rewarded" with a small promotion and practically no salary increase. Now that she has the privilege of being exempt, she receives no overtime pay for her extra work. According to her, there was nowhere else for her to be promoted to and she had reached the top of her pay scale—her salary increases were minimal. She was angry, felt taken advantage of, and was in no mood to put in a lot of overtime.

Who was right? There is no way to answer that question without knowing more of the specific details of her work. What is obvious from these conversations, however, is that the rules in this company are geared toward productivity. "Get the work done no matter what it takes to do it." I asked her if she thought that this statement was one of the company's rules of the game, and she quickly agreed that it certainly was. My advice to her was to not kid herself. If productivity at all costs is a company rule, she either needs to follow it or leave. Although we discussed ways she could negotiate for some of the benefits or salary changes that she wanted, she was quite certain that negotiation would be useless,that the company did not care.

In contrast, I know many managers who are famous for combining an intense commitment to their employees' welfare with the unyielding rule, "We work until the job is done, no matter what it takes." As with all tribal values, it is possible to combine beliefs that on the surface seem contradictory. To do so, you must really believe those values and work hard to develop tribal or organizational rules that provide clear guidelines to employees for their behavior. Modeling those rules by your own behavior and continually communicating with the tribes and employees about their importance are the two best strategies for producing the results you want.

Other Common Rules of the Game

Here are a few additional rules that are difficult to match with a specific value. The values they reflect depend on the company and on the situation. In fact, different tribes may have the same rule but define its meaning differently, depending on the value it is associated with. Look these over, and see if any of them sound familiar:

"Shoot from the hip."
"Meet the deadline at all costs."
"Do it right the first time and save time later fixing it."
"We work better under pressure."
"Dive in headfirst."
"Inch into the water carefully."
"NIH (Not Invented Here)—so don't support it."
"If we aren't having a good time around here, something is wrong with
     the way we are doing the work."

As you can see, there is an endless list of possible rules of the game. Identifying those of the tribes in your organization is what is important.

IDENTIFYING YOUR TRIBAL RULES OF THE GAME

Sometimes it is easier to identify tribal rules other than your own. Their mottoes have been a continual source of irritation to you in the past, so you are painfully aware of the rules they work by. Your own rules are so rational and organic that it is difficult to see them.

Start by identifying what you often say to each other about your own tribe's work or about the other tribes. This exercise will uncover some of your tribal mottoes. Articulating what it is that the other tribes are not doing that you wish they would do may tell you some of your tribe's rules. For example, the tribes in charge of handling paperwork will often complain that other tribes never get the paperwork in on time and forget to fill out half of what is needed when they finally do show up with it. Their own rules are buried in these complaints—accuracy, do it right the first time, meeting deadlines at all costs. But these are clearly not important rules for some of the other tribes.

Another way to discover your own rules is to list a number of complaints that other tribes in the organization have about your tribe. Respond to each of these criticisms with, "Yes, but. . .". Your defense will probably be an eloquent description of one of your tribal rules. For example, Manufacturing, Distribution, and Engineering complain to Sales that it should not be selling new products that have not made it through the design, testing, and initial production phases. The sales tribe responds, "Yes, but our customers are asking for it now. Besides, you guys are too slow." The sales tribal rules, "Tell the customer what he wants to hear," and, "Speed at all costs," are evident in that response.

Once you have identified a few of the rules of the game for several of your organization's tribes, put them side by side and notice the differences. All you have to do is glance over these juxtaposed rules to see that you could write the scripts for the tribal arguments that are likely to occur when the rules bump into each other. On the average, rules produce more humor, but also more conflict, than any other tribal characteristic.

GOOD AND BAD RULES OF THE GAME

For the most part, these descriptions of the various tribal rules have been neutral. The decision about which rules are good for the organization and which ones are not is an internal company decision and a customer decision. A rule such as, "Speed at all costs," could be very useful to a tribe and appropriate for an organization—or it could be a disaster. It depends on the situation and on how the rule governs specific behaviors.

You could take almost any rule and develop both a positive and a negative story about the effect it could have on an organization.

There are a few guidelines to follow when deciding whether a rule is good or bad for the organization. First, you should be able to connect each rule to one of the organization's umbrella values. If tribal values and rules do not fit under an umbrella value of the organization, they may be dangerous. "Shoot from the hip," for instance, could be a free-floating rule that has no connection to any organizational umbrella value. Perhaps it was an outgrowth of individual personalities, but it may not be useful to the company. On the other hand, in a fast-paced, entrepreneurial company, this rule might fit well under the umbrella values of adventure, flexibility, responsiveness, and creativity.

Rules are very difficult to manage or legislate away. Ordering a tribe to "quit doing that" may cause them to hide their tactics, but it will rarely change their rules. The CEO in one of my client companies was telling me about irritating tactics used by the sales force. The sales tribe is supposed to rely on written and telephone communications with specialist tribes for technical updates on the products. One group of salespeople, however, is located in the same building and on the same floor with some of the specialist tribes. They find it quicker and more expedient to "drop in" to ask questions of the specialists, or to even poke through the papers on the specialists' desks.

This, of course, is very annoying to the specialist tribes. The CEO has sent several memos to the sales force telling them to stay out of the spe-cialists' areas. This is a "loose" entrepreneurial, organization, and the CEO is the first to admit that his directive memos are not likely to bring the organization to a screeching halt to salute him in obedience. But it is irritating to him that the sales force seemed to have paid no attention to this particular request. We talked about the sales tribe's rules on speed and snooping around for new ideas. We decided that the only thing that would stop their forays into specialist territory would be for him to move his own desk and park it in the middle of the specialist entrance. That might work, but I have my doubts. Many of the salespeople will probably wave and yell hello to the CEO as they charge onto specialist turf. Moving them across town would probably be the only foolproof way to stop them.

Another issue to consider when deciding whether the rules are good or bad for your organization is their flexibility. If many of the tribal rules are very specific and are narrowly defined—one right way to do things—there is not much room for adjusting when necessary. Flexibility in using the rules is another way to make them work effectively. One organization that I worked with was trying to become more customer responsive. The employees in several tribes pointed out to me that they had been thoroughly trained on what the rules were. But they had received no training on when they could bend the rules, or even ignore them, to please a customer. Very few individuals were willing to take the personal risk of breaking a rule unless they had been told that they had some flexibility and had been given examples of when to follow and when to ignore particular rules.

Another basic question to ask about any tribal rule is whether or not it is ethical. Lying to customers, fudging the numbers, or claiming credit for successes that you or your tribe did not achieve are examples of rules that are clearly unethical. But the ethicalness of many rules depends on how they are used. If your organization has lofty-sounding values, but many unethical rules, the mixed messages will eventually get through to employees, customers, and the public. The research on ethics indicates that in most situations people know the difference between right and wrong. The question is: Are they *doing* what they know to be right? Tribal rules are one place to look when considering the question of whether your organization has ethical practices.

NOT ALL RULES ARE CREATED EQUAL

The rules of different tribes can, of course, come into conflict, but the rules within one tribe can also clash at times. For example, a tribe may have the rules:

- Move as fast as you can and keep going

- Do a quality job the first time

- Please the customer

Ideally, the tribal members abide by all three rules at the same time by producing fast, high-quality work that pleases the customer. But following the rules is not always that simple. The tribe may have a particularly demanding customer whose standards are difficult to meet and who asks it to do the work over again. Another customer may want some special service that will take more time than usual. If the tribal member is faced with these situations and does not know which rule to follow and which to sacrifice, he is left to make his own judgment call.

Usually, the rules attached to the most important umbrella values will be the ones that have the highest priority. If the most important value for the company is providing excellent customer service, then the rule, "Please the customer," will take priority. The employee should be able to make that decision with confidence that he will be supported for it. If, on the other hand, being a fast-paced, high-profit company is really the overriding value, the employee could actually get into trouble for responding to the customers' demands for custom service or for redoing the job. Where pride in quality craftsmanship or technical skills is high, the rule, "Do a quality job the first time," takes priority. Enforcing this rule could result in the tribal member informing the customer that he does not know what he is talking about—the work is right the way it is. Professional tribes commonly take that stance—architects, doctors, or my own tribe, consultants. If the customer does not like the work the way the professional did it, then the customer either has no taste, is ignorant, or lacks good judgment. The tribe's own definition of quality takes priority over the rule of pleasing the customer.

The SAS flight attendant who decided to go around the catering supervisor to get more food for her passengers clearly knew which SAS rule to follow. "Pleasing the customers" took priority over "Rules are rules." She was certainly supported for knowing that when the CEO of SAS, Jan Carlzon, chose her story as one to include in his book, *Moments of Truth*. Not many employees get written up for worldwide reading as a reward for following the right rule; fortunately, there are simpler ways to let the tribes know that they are choosing the right rule to enforce.

What tribal members are sometimes trying to say when they insist that their tribe is right and another is wrong is that their rules should take priority. This may be true in some cases. The customer-oriented tribe, for example, really may call the shots in a very sales-oriented company. I am usually skeptical, however, when the conflict over priorities occurs *between* tribes. They are each so used to thinking that they are right and everyone else is wrong that often neither of their judgment calls in these situations reflects organizational values. The safest approach is to assume that the best solution is to combine rules, that the two tribes need to compromise. If one tribe's rule is to take priority, then that decision should be made by a top-management person who can see the big picture and focus on the organization's umbrella values. This decision can include guidelines so that the tribes do not have to come back to ask management to referee every time they come up against a similar situation. One caution, however: if the senior management person making this decision came up through the ranks of one particular tribe, then he is very likely to be almost as biased as the current tribal members. Management people who have moved around the organization, in and out of many different tribes, are less likely to have this natural bias. But anyone choosing which rules take priority needs to be sure that his decision is in line with the organization's umbrella values, that it does not reflect a personal preference for one rule or the other, or for one tribe or another.

QUESTIONS TO ASK ABOUT YOUR TRIBAL RULES OF THE GAME

What are your tribal Mottoes? The examples listed earlier in this chapter may help to remind you. If you have a hard time thinking of your tribe's mottoes, make a point of listening to your fellow members during the coming days. If you can detach yourself and think like an anthropologist, you will begin to hear the often repeated mottoes of your tribe. If you are really stumped on your own tribe, see if you can hear some mottoes of other tribes. It is often easier to take the anthropological view of other groups than it is to look at your own that way.

What are those other tribes not doing that you wish they would do? The other tribes tend to irritate you when they are not following your rules. Perhaps you value accuracy and they constantly make mistakes in detail work or do not even do the detail work. "Satisfy the customer" is one of your key rules, but another tribe refuses to get on the phone to explain to the customer some technical information that you don't understand in detail yourself. All you hear is, "Talking to the customers is *your* job." But when other tribes will not do things you wish they would do, chances are that you are trying to get them to follow your tribal rules, at the expense of their own.

List several criticisms that other tribes would have about your tribe. *What is your response to each of their criticisms?* Your "yes, but. . ." defense will probably contain at least one of your rules. If you really get on a roll, you may end up discovering several rules articulated in defense of just one criticism. Have some fun with this one—the more eloquent and dramatic you get in your tribal defense, the more the rules will surface.

Look back at some of the key values you came up with in Chapter 4, both tribal and umbrella values. Take each value and think of several rules that are direct spin-offs from it. Now look back at some of the rules you came up with from the mottoes, irritations, and defenses in the questions above. Determine which values go with each of these rules, keeping in mind that some rules may go with several values.

Step back and take a look at the big picture for your organization. *Are your umbrella values in sync with the rules and day-to-day behavior of your tribes?* Does management say that people are the company's greatest asset, but then follow rules signifying that human resources are an expensive overhead item to be reduced wherever possible? Do you have the umbrella value that everything revolves around the customer, but one review of recent customer complaints tells you that the customers feel overcharged, underserviced, and lied to by some of your tribes? Do you say that your company thrives on innovation, but the employees laugh at the idea that anyone is really interested in their ideas? If there are gaps between your stated values and the rules as reflected in employees' day-to-day behavior, people inside and outside the company will believe the rules and behavior, not the values written on a piece of paper or delivered in a dramatic speech.

How flexible are the rules in your organization? Do people know when to follow them and when to break them? Is there one right way to do things, or a lot of options to choose from, depending on the situation? Would anyone at a front-line level dare to end-run a supervisor in the way that the SAS flight attendant did when she knew the rule she was following was more important to the company than the supervisor's rule?

This is a tough question to ask. *Are any of the rules in your various tribes unethical?* Answering it is usually fairly easy, but facing up to the answer and doing something about it can be tough.

If your company is working hard on developing a strategic plan that is forward-thinking and flexible, watch out for tribal rules. *Do a "rules check" to see if any of the established behaviors of the tribes are in conflict with your strategic plan.* If you find conflict, confront it and discuss it with the tribes. Involve them in developing new rules and behaviors that match the strategic plan. Don't kid yourself that a management mandate to "quit doing that!" will change anything. Usually all that accomplishes is sending the tribes underground with their rules. You cannot see the rules as easily, but they are still there.

List several of your own tribe's key rules. *What are the situations in which you might have to choose one and sacrifice another?*

- Speed

- Quality

- Customer satisfaction

- Cost control

- Accuracy

Which one of the above factors takes priority in your tribe? Why? What umbrella value is your highest priority rule tied to, making it more important than the others?

If the clash of rules in your organization between tribes, be careful about the kind of thinking that leads you to conclude that your own tribe is obviously right and that your rule is the one to take priority over all other tribes' rules. Remember the umbrella values of your organization and try to find a joint solution, which is most likely to be best for the organization.

II HOW TO BUILD BRIDGES BETWEEN TRIBES

8 MIGRATING SKILLS

The North Andamen Islanders have a peace-making ceremony . . . [in which] dancers from two contending factions mingle randomly to form two groups, each new group consisting of about equal numbers from each faction. One group of dancers then acts out their feelings of aggression by violently shaking the members of the other group. In response, members of the second group show complete passivity, expressing neither fear nor resentment. Using this ceremony, collective anger is appeased, wrongs are forgiven, and peace is temporarily restored.[1]

Wouldn't it be nice if it was that easy in organizations? I must admit that this description conjures up images for me of the finance tribe and the designers tribe in ritual dance with each other, or maybe the sales force and the manufacturing tribe. I cannot picture, however, either group standing still passively and allowing itself to be violently shaken by the other group. There are some rituals, however, that are more likely to work with the kinds of tribes that you find in organizations.

The first step in bridging the tribal gap—and probably the most important one—is to recognize the different tribal "realities." The first section of this book has outlined the characteristics of organizational tribes, giving you a blueprint to follow in looking at your own tribes. The ability to describe other tribes' points of view is an essential first step in building communication bridges between the groups. It is not important whether the tribes agree with or even understand each other's realities. But it is possible for everyone to be aware that the tribes are different—and for good reasons—and that differences do not necessarily make other tribes wrong.

Occasionally, you will have crossover members, people who have been members of two or more tribes in the organization and who truly understand and even agree with more than one tribal reality. These people can be very helpful in bridging the gaps as long as their diplomacy skills are strong enough to keep them from having everyone angry at them most of the time. Crossover tribal members play a rewarding but hazardous role. Often an organization uses outside, temporary consultants for this role. If your organization has few of these internal diplomats, they are a valuable resource worth protecting and using.

The second step in building the communication bridges is using what I call "migrating" skills. These are the communication skills needed to link what you are saying with the other person's point of view in a way that is likely to produce a negotiated agreement. This chapter will focus on individual, one-on-one conversation between members of different tribes. Migrating skills help you know what to say and when to say it to bridge the gap and produce satisfying results for both tribes.

ANATOMY OF A CONVERSATION

To understand how migrating skills work, it is necessary to know the basic structure of a conversation between two people. There are two elements to a conversation, and both play a role in bridging any communication gap. The first is the "transaction" topic of the conversation. The problem to be solved, the information to be gathered, the question to be answered—these are examples of transactions. Most experienced employees have a high level of transaction expertise.

The second element is usually less obvious to the participants because it is in the background. The "relationship" element is not *what* you are talking about, but *how* you are talking about it. Although "relationship" is not the focus or purpose of the conversation, it will usually have the greater long-term consequences. Most employees have far less expertise in handling this communication element than the transaction element. They often say, "I don't have time to fool with that." All they want is to get through the transaction as quickly as possible, without worrying about the effect it has on their relationship with the person they are talking to. Whether they have time or not, some relationship always exists between two people in a conversation, and this relationship is affected by what happens in the conversation. There is no way to escape it.

There are four ways to handle the relationship aspect of a conversation:

1. You can *build* the relationship. This is likely to occur during the first conversations between two individuals, as they get to know each other and form a solid base for future transactions.
2. You can *protect* the relationship. This occurs after a positive relationship has already been established. At the end of any conversation, you are no better off and no worse off than you were before. Protection is not a neutral or passive act; to maintain or protect the relationship entails deliberate actions.
3. You can *repair* the relationship. This occurs when there have been problems between two people in the past. Repair of a relationship is usually a very slow process. With each conversation, you inch your way back to a better relationship.
4. You can *damage* the relationship. If you do not build, protect, or repair a relationship, then damage occurs by default. "I don't have time to worry about the relationship" translates into damage. With each conversation that causes damage, it becomes more and more difficult to use any of the other three alternatives effectively. If the damage goes beyond two individuals and becomes the standard communication pattern between all tribal members, then the result will be tribal warfare.

MIGRATING

Migrating is the ability to link two tribes together in both the transaction and relationship elements of communication. What you say will address the topic of the conversation, and how you say it—the timing, the word choices, the order of your statements—will address the relationship. The goal of migrating is to create a balanced outcome in which each tribe has its point of view taken into consideration and incorporated into the results of the conversation. All "win-win" negotiation skills are forms of migrating. What often is missing, however, is tribal knowledge. If you think you are simply negotiating in a vacuum, between two individuals, you are likely to end up with both people angry and with no solution to the problem. Knowing that you are negotiating with an individual who is also a tribal representative will help you see more clearly what the other side needs and will give you more alternatives for meeting those needs as well as your own. As Fred Jandt and Paul Gillette say in their book, *Win-Win Negotiating,* "The greater the number of issues that two negotiators can identify, the more room there is to structure an outcome in which both can perceive themselves as winners."[2]

The four steps listed below are what highly skilled negotiators do sentence by sentence in a conversation. This process reflects an attitude and a rhythm of thinking, that can become automatic with practice.

Step One.   Be sure you know something about the other person's tribal reality. If you don't, either try to ask some questions and find out on the spot or proceed with caution. Lacking any tribal knowledge is like trying to negotiate in a foreign country where you don't speak the language. Use the questions on the five tribal characteristics in the first section of this book as guidelines on the kinds of questions to ask yourself about the other person's tribe. Asking the other person what he thinks might be a solution, and why he thinks that approach might work, will often give you some insight into his tribal values and priorities. It will tell you what is important to him about the issue. Asking him questions about how he might want to go about implementing his ideas will often give you some information about his tribe's rules of the game as well. You will know more about the tactics and strategies his tribe is likely to use. As he talks, you can listen for cues on language, thinking pattern, and background.

Step Two.   Listen to what the other person is saying and identify the key topic in his comments. What is he talking about? What is the transaction from his point of view? This will be an educated guess on your part, but don't worry—if you guess wrong, he will let you know in a hurry. Sometimes the topic is actually a feeling he is expressing, rather than factual content.

Step Three.   Identify your own (or your tribe's) goal for this conversation. It is important for you to know more about your side of the story than just the topic. You need to be clear about what you want out of this conversation. What needs are you trying to meet? What action are you trying to accomplish? The goal might be as simple as, "to end this damn conversation as quickly as possible." But other examples of goals might be solving a problem, making a sale, or agreeing on the next step in a project that you are working on jointly.

Step Four.   When you have identified the other person's topic, link that topic with your goal immediately, in the next remark you make. Acknowledge his topic first, and then tie it to your goal. This can usually be done in one, or at most two, sentences. (See Figure 8–1.) Often the easiest way to start a migrating sentence is with the phrase, "I understand. . . ," followed by something indicating that you were listening to what he just said to you. Bring in your goal by explaining your side of the story. In other words, *migrate first,* and then bring him back to your turf. He will be much more willing to hear what you have to say if he feels that he has been listened to and understood.

If you follow these steps sentence by sentence, correcting course whenever you guess wrong on the topic, the odds are that you will reach a balanced outcome in which everyone wins because you will have linked your two perspectives to find solutions that meet both your needs. No negotiating strategy guarantees success. But if migrating doesn't work, nothing is going to work! Notice there are no boxing punches in this approach. If the other person throws one, you simply

Figure 8–1.   Linking Goals and Topics.

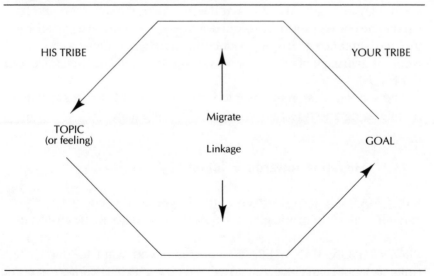

HIS TRIBE

YOUR TRIBE

TOPIC
(or feeling)

Migrate

Linkage

GOAL

ignore it and pick up on his topic. You then respond to that topic by migrating and linking it to your goal. For him, it will be like trying to box with a person using judo. The punches never land anywhere.

I have worked with many groups as they practice this skill. One person will play the "other" tribe and start talking about a typical problem or concern from that tribe's point of view. I then have several people throw out their responses, then ask each to explain what he heard as the topic and what his goal was in his response. The first person then tells us which respondent (if any) came the closest to hearing his topic accurately and was most successful in closing the gap. Almost always, people are extremely skillful at knowing their own goals (step three), but are amateurs at hearing the topics or feelings in the other person's comments (step two). Sometimes I cannot even get the respondents to answer the question, "What was the topic?" When asked, they keep repeating their own goal. I am convinced that they are not trying to be difficult. They simply do not know what the other tribe's topic was.

SAMPLE CONVERSATION

This sample conversation is adapted from a real one that took place between the sales manager and the production manager of a video production company. In the first version of the conversation, you will see the good migrating skills that the production manager could have used. The conversation is broken down to show you the topic and goal in each sentence that the production manager might have uttered. Notice that in each of his responses he migrates first, and then goes back to his goal.

The second version is closer to how the conversation really went— no migrating and no solution, a verbal boxing match.

Migrating Toward a Solution

SALES MANAGER: "I need a firm finish date on those new videos so I can start selling them and give accurate delivery dates to the customers."

PRODUCTION MANAGER: "I understand you want to start selling (migrate), but I can't give you an exact date yet" (goal). (*Sales topic:* The production manager's guess as to the sales manager's topic was that he wants to start selling. *Production Goal:* To not get locked in to an exact date that he may not be able to meet.)

SALES MANAGER: "But the customers are going to ask about delivery and I've got to tell them something. Last time I guessed on a delivery date and I was wrong. I had both you and the customers at my throat. Now, what am I going to tell them this time? Here's your chance—tell me a date or I'll just have to do the best I can without you. I can't wait."

PRODUCTION MANAGER: "Okay, you need to tell the customers something (migrate) and I need to keep the schedule flexible because I can't predict every glitch we may run into between now and then (goal). How about if you give the customers a time range for when the videos will be delivered. I can give you four-to-six-week time span and feel safe that we'll make it. Will that work for you?" (*Sales topic:* The salesman has to tell the customers something about dates. *Production goal:* Same as before—not to get locked into an exact date that he can't meet.)

SALES MANAGER: "Well, it's not great. Can't you get any more specific than that?"

PRODUCTION MANAGER: "If you want a more specific date (migrate), you'll have to wait another month (goal). Then I'll be able to give you a range of two to three weeks. But if you want to start selling now, I need four to six weeks to work with. I can go either way—which is better for you?" (*Sales topic:* A narrower range of dates. *Production goal:* Not to give a narrower range of dates at this point.)

SALES MANAGER: "Give me the four-to-six-week range, and I'll go with it. Let me know as soon as you know a more specific time line."

The production manager could have demonstrated these skills:

- Migrating in each response

- Migrating first then tying the topic to his goal

- Never budging an inch from his main goal, but still negotiating in

each sentence by suggesting alternatives that linked the sales topic
and his production goal

- Used several alternatives that the sales manager could pick from, all
  of which would meet his goal

- Ensuring that both tribes went away at least partially satisfied and
  unlikely to renege on the deal (win-win)

A Boxing Match Instead

SALES MANAGER: "I need a firm finish date on those new videos so I
can start selling them and give accurate delivery dates to the customers."

PRODUCTION MANAGER: "I can't give it to you, we don't know yet"
(no migrating).

SALES MANAGER: "What do you mean, you can't give it to me? I've got
to be able to tell the customers something. What am I supposed to do—
just sit on my hands while you guys play MGM?" (boxing punch).

PRODUCTION MANAGER: "Look, I told you—I don't have dates yet"
(no migrating). "You'll just have to wait. And don't go making up dates
like you did last time! You make us all look like a bunch of idiots!"
(counter punch).

SALES MANAGER: "Oh yeah, and sitting around twiddling our thumbs
with no sales coming in makes us look like geniuses, I suppose!"
(phone slams down).

   No one won that round. They had a boxing match that will probably
lead to tribal warfare unless someone else intervenes. Sales loses,
Production loses, and ultimately the customer will probably lose too.

GENERATING ALTERNATIVE SOLUTIONS

After you migrate to the other person's turf and let him know that you
heard the point he was making, you should link that point to your own

goal. If you do not, you are losing control of the conversation and will not accomplish your goal. The main skill involved in linking the other side's topic to your goal is the ability to think of alternative solutions. This often requires quick thinking on your feet as well as practice, to do well.

There are a few guidelines to follow as you work on your "linkage" skills. *Any* alternative you suggest should at least partially meet your goal. There is no point in throwing out suggestions that would not accomplish what you want. To be able to do this, you had better be sure that you *know* what you want. Ask yourself quickly what it is that you or your tribe is trying to accomplish in this situation, and give yourself several answers to that question, if possible. The more familiar you are with your tribe's goal, the better a job you will do in thinking up alternatives that will achieve it.

The second guideline to keep in mind is to not get locked into one specific solution—either it has to be done exactly this way or you will fight. There is almost always more than one way to meet your goal. If you trap yourself into thinking there is only one right method for achieving your goal, then you increase the odds considerably that you will lose completely. Using the Production-Sales dialogues when the sales manager insisted on a solution that gave him one specific finish date now, he did not have a prayer of winning. At the same time, when the production manager determined that the only acceptable solution for him was no commitment to any dates, he was inviting the sales manager to go out and make up dates again. Each needed to be willing to look at a few alternative solutions that would have been compromises between the two extreme positions.

There is a great difference between collaboration and compromise. In general, *collaboration* means that both sides try to find a solution that fully meets both sets of goals. Everyone wins completely. *Compromise* means that the two sides meet in the middle, both giving up a few things but still getting enough of their goals met to be satisfied. The first Production-Sales dialogue was an example of compromise. In disputes between tribes with very different values and rules of the game, you are usually going to have to settle for compromise. But do not forget that collaboration is possible. If you generate alternative solutions well enough, you may end up with everyone winning 100 percent of their goals more often than you thought could be possible.

Collaboration is the highest skill level in the art of negotiating. You probably have a few people in your organization who are naturally good at it. But as a consultant who spends a great deal of time working with organizational tribes to help them develop their migrating and linking skills, I will gladly settle for compromise level skills. A verbal boxing match is the strategy to be avoided.

Two Ears and One Mouth for a Reason!

When you were a child, did you ever hear this expression? God gave you two ears and one mouth for a reason. If people learned to listen and talk in approximately that ratio, we would all be better at migrating and negotiating. To learn about another tribe's topics and know how to migrate, you have to listen first and talk later. It is often a good idea to listen twice as much as you talk. If you listen enough to know as much about another person's topic as you do about your goal, it does not take much talking on your part to link the two together and get the outcome you want. You end up with better results and shorter conversations by listening more effectively.

Nowhere is this more important than in handling a conversation in which the other person is angry. This is a negotiation situation with the heat turned up under it. When the other person is venting his anger, you must listen and stay in migrating gear until he begins to calm down. During this phase you should never say anything more complicated than, "Oh, I see," or, "I understand." Any effort to get him to move to your turf while he is still angry is like throwing gasoline on a fire. Such an effort would make him more angry, leading him to vent his feelings at a louder volume for a longer time. No matter how good your intentions, if you try to win him over to your solution too soon, he will use your comments to get even angrier.

It is the rhythm of the conversation that creates bridges. Migrate . . . link . . . migrate . . . link—building the bridges with each response. Most people and tribes respond quite well to this approach. But if you stand firmly on your tribal turf, reach across the gap, and try to jerk them over to your side, warfare is the most likely outcome.

QUESTIONS TO ASK ABOUT MIGRATING

What are the guerrilla warfare tactics between the tribes in your organization? If you are the CEO of your company, you probably do not know the answer to that question. You are the last person they want to know about the tactics they are using! In your case, you will probably need to think back and remember the guerrilla tactics you used in earlier days. Everyone else in the organization should have no trouble knowing what their guerrilla tactics are.

In an intertribal conflict or problem that you have been personally involved in recently, what was your goal in the situation? Try to come up with several different ways of answering that question. If you can remember any of the conversation between you and the other tribe's representative, what do you think was the topic in the statements that person was making? If you cannot remember the other person's side of the conversation well enough to answer that question, ask yourself if you were really listening. When people repeat a story about a confrontation they had with someone else, they can usually repeat verbatim every word they said themselves—"and then I said. . .". Often their memories are not so clear about the other side of the conversation, which was just the stage setting for their own brilliant comments.

Take that same situation and now try to generate at least five alternative solutions. Make sure that each one at least partially satisfies your goal. If you cannot do it, get someone to help you. Learning to come up with alternative ideas is a skill that takes practice. There are always people in an organization who have a natural talent for generating alternatives. Have one of them help you practice until you are good at thinking quickly on your feet. In most tribal confrontations, you do not have time to go away and ponder the situation. You are on the spot and must respond immediately.

Try to think of an example of collaboration and an example of compromise from your past experiences with intertribal problem-solving. The compromises will probably be the easiest for you to recall. Collaborations do not happen as often; they usually surprise both of you as you discover that you can each get what you want out of the situation. Collaborations are fairly rare but well worth looking for in your negotiation efforts.

Think back to a time when someone was angry at you. What amount of time did you spend listening to what the person was saying, and what amount talking? Did you listen first and talk second? Usually, you will know if you talked too much, and too soon, because the other person gets angrier and angrier as the conversation proceeds. If the angry person calmed down fairly quickly and was soon willing to rationally discuss the situation, you probably did a very good job of listening and riding the anger wave before you started talking.

9 SKILLS FOR HANDLING TRIBAL STRESS

There are many sources of stress in a work setting and conflict between tribes ranks high on the list of ulcer-producing events for most employees. Knowledge of other tribes is the first step to reducing this stress; knowing why people act the way they do makes them more predictable. Stress can be looked at from either an individual or organizational point of view. In this chapter, both perspectives will be addressed.

STRESS-RESISTANT PEOPLE

New research in the past few years has looked at stress-resistant behavior and attitudes for individuals: Why do people experiencing the same kind of stressful events in their lives react react in different ways? Some people become upset, get sick, or burn out. Others seem unaffected, or even seem to thrive. They can resist the stressors around them. People who are stress-resistant are the same people who are consistently rated the peak performers in organizations. Researchers characterize the attitudes of these stress-resistant individuals in the following ways.

Commitment. "Loving what you are doing and doing what you love. It is knowing what you want, honoring your innermost desires and translating them into action."[1] Strongly committed people find it easy to be interested in whatever they are doing and can involve themselves in it wholeheartedly. Commitment contrasts with alienation, which is a characteristic of people who find things boring or meaningless and who hang back from involvement in the tasks they have to do.[2] James Loehr, who works with professional and Olympic athletes, says that one of the first questions he asks an athlete is, "Are you having fun with your sport?" If the athlete says, "No, I used to love it, but not anymore," Loehr knows that athlete has a long way to go toward achieving peak perform-ance[3]

Commitment is a characteristic that is closely linked to tribal values. If the individual's values are compatible with the organization's, work-related commitment will be a much easier attitude to acquire and main-tain. An organization cannot, however, create employee commitment. This is something that comes only from inside the individual, even though it can flourish in a supportive setting.

Confidence. "Confidence doesn't depend upon your performance, nor does it fluctuate with other people's moods, how you look or the political climate in your office. It is the constant positive experience of yourself that is not dependent upon anything external."[4] Fear is a major obstacle to confidence. The opposite of confidence is feeling threatened and fearing change.[5] Stress-resistant people will tell you that mistakes and failures are not obstacles. It is the *fear* of mistakes and failures that will increase your stress and decrease your performance.

In any organization you can identify the people with high levels of confidence by the way they handle risk. Effective risk-takers are willing to take risks that have a reasonable likelihood of successful outcomes and that they have investigated carefully before "the leap." These people usually have high confidence levels. They have a good batting average on successful risk-taking and recover relatively easily when things do not work out as well as anticipated. Occasional failures are in-evitable to these people, but they learn from failure, which, to them, is the stepping stone to future success.

Control. "Something is not in your control if it is externally influenced. Ultimately, the only thing you can control is yourself—your own thoughts, feelings, attitudes and actions."[6] Stress-resistant employees are able to look at a problem or challenge and answer three questions about it:

1. What can I control in this situation? (What can I personally make happen by my own actions?)
2. What can I influence in this situation? (What can I do to "nudge" the situation in the direction I want it to move in? What can I persuade other people to do?)
3. What factors in this situation do I have no control over? (What is it that I can neither do myself nor influence others to do?)

Once the stress-resistant answer these three questions, they focus all their energy and activity on the items they can control or influence. They do not waste any of their energy on the factors they have no control over. Considering how economically they use their time and energy, it is no mystery why they are peak performers. They use their energy in ways that produce results. Spending energy on trying to affect what is out of your control is like beating your head against the proverbial brick wall. The wall does not fall down, but you end up with one heck of a headache! And with no peak performance, but a great deal of stress.

Nevertheless many employees at all levels in organizations spend a great deal of time focusing on "no control" factors: griping in the bathroom, complaining over lunch, gossiping, arguing over policies, and emotionally resisting and fighting the inevitable. For example, a few years ago the health care industry experienced some major regulatory changes that were triggered by the federal government's changes in Medicare reimbursement. Once these new laws had been passed, there was no question but that they had to be implemented. They were a fact of life that had to be faced. Having no control over the regulations themselves, hospitals tried to exert a great deal of control and influence by the ways in which they carried out these new regulations. Some hospitals took the "drag us into this kicking and screaming" approach; others seemed to say, "Okay, what can we do to make this work as well as possible for us?" These are very different ways of using energy and resources. I am certain that it is not difficult to guess which hospitals are doing better at this point in time. You cannot perform at your best when you are wasting time and energy on fighting battles that cannot be won.

One result of focusing on "no control" items is that you are distracted and miss opportunities to act in the areas you can control. I fall into this trap easily when I am in airports commuting around the country. I have no control over flight schedules, delays, lost baggage, and so on. But I want to have control over these things so badly that I often end up focusing on them and burn up energy being angry. In the meantime, I fail to notice the things I can control or influence. For example, last year I was flying home from a trip to New Jersey. I finished my work early and arrived at Newark Airport about four hours before my flight was scheduled to leave. I was tired and irritated at the long wait, so I stewed around grumbling and complaining to myself. I sat there and fantasized about being the CEO of an airline and "fixing" all these problems. Finally the time passed, and I was within forty-five minutes of boarding the plane. I guess my mind started to relax, because suddenly it occurred to me that Newark was not the only airport in the New York area. I grabbed my flight schedule book and quickly realized that there had been a flight from the other airport that I could have caught. If I had gotten that flight, I would have been driving into my garage at home right about then. I spent my energy focusing on the "no control" factors in my situation and missed an opportunity to act on a "control" factor. My reward: three extra hours of frustration sitting in an airport, and arriving home worn out.

Tribal warfare is often focused on "no control" factors. Tribes argue with each other and complain about the inevitable differences between them. They use their energy trying to get other tribes to change. In the meantime, they spend very little energy on migrating and negotiating. The results are poor performance on all sides and soaring stress levels. Effective cross-tribal communication does not eliminate the differences between tribes. Negotiating between tribes does take a lot of energy, but it produces the best results possible and lowers the stress levels of everyone involved as much as possible.

Organizations can be stress-producing or stress-resistant in much the same way that individuals can. Organizations need to clarify their commitments to key values and directions. Without this clarity, it is difficult for managers, tribes, or individual employees to feel any sense of control over their work.

STRESS-RESISTANT ORGANIZATIONS

Many times when I am brought into an organization to assist in improving teamwork between the tribes, I find individuals who are very committed to their own tribe and to the organization. This is especially true for longtime employees. What I also find, however, is that they have often lost sight of just exactly what it is they are committed to! The company has changed, the environment in which they do business has changed, and their senior management may have changed also. The loyal and committed employees no longer have a clear picture of the priorities of the organization and often cannot even tell me what the company's specific "line of business" is anymore. Sometimes the customer base has shifted, and they are not even sure who the target audience for their products and services is. These are committed people, but with no clear sense of direction. They are willing to work hard to make the company great. But their question for me is, "Great at what?"

What is usually happening in a directionless situation is that managers, front-line employees, and tribes take on lots of projects, goals, and plans and treat all of them as top priority. In other words, they do not focus on any one or two particular priorities and organize their energy and resources around those priorities. They treat *everything* as a key issue and spread their energy and resources thin. In the inevitable crisis mode that results, they choose their "priorities" according to which issue or problem is grabbing their time and attention. They often tell me that they feel like they are running fast and going nowhere. And to a great extent, they are right. This kind of shotgun use of an organization's energy rarely produces the best quality results. What it does produce is very high stress levels for everyone in the organization. After a few months (or years, for the die-hards), these people burn out and many of them leave the organization. Or they just quit caring anymore. Commitment needs a clear-cut cause, or it dies.

One of the reasons for lack of direction seems to be the fast pace of change. It is no longer possible to set your direction and maintain that same focus year after year. The environment, customers, and competition demand constant updating of the organization's direction. Most organizations cannot meet all the demands or take advantage of all the opportunities in their markets. There is simply too much going on to be able to do everything. But rather than make the hard choices and pick their niches, organizations stretch themselves too thin and try to take on too much. When I hear constant references to overload, exhaustion, confusion, poor planning, and so forth, I often find that the organization has dozens of issues and priorities that it is trying to address all at the same time. Everyone from the president to the newest front-line employee races around with that unmistakable "high blood pressure look" on their faces.

The 80/20 Principle

There are many ways to focus the direction of an organization, and a number of suggestions are given in Chapter 4. Umbrella values that are clearly understood can provide the basic direction for a company. Another way to narrow the focus of an organization is to apply the "80/20 principle" at all levels, from senior management to the tribes. Simply put, the 80/20 principle is that you get 80 percent of your good results out of only 20 percent of your activity. Therefore, if you want to focus your energy in the most productive way, you must identify the 20 percent of your daily, weekly, or yearly activities that produce 80 percent of your results. After you identify the crucial 20 percent, you organize your to-do list, your budget, your personnel, and every other resource you have to maximize that 20 percent.

This does *not* mean that you ignore or discard the rest of your responsibilities—that less productive 80 percent. You probably cannot do that. It does mean that you eliminate as much of the 80 percent as you can, and then you spend less of your resources on what must remain on your agenda. You do not do everything that comes your way with an even distribution of energy and concentration. People who tell me proudly that they "give their all to everything they do" are often telling me that, with their efforts so diluted, their results are less than they could be. They are almost always telling me that they are exhausted most of the time.

Even though the 80/20 way of thinking about priorities is obviously better for everyone's health and also makes sense as a way to manage resources, most people in organizations are unable to apply it. In my work, I ask many groups of managers or tribes to look back over the past week or month of their business activity and to divide their work into these two categories—the 20 percent that's important and the 80 percent that can wait. Often I can persuade or pressure them into doing it in the workshop setting, but I find that it is often difficult to get them to truly start thinking about their work routinely in an 80/20 format. They keep telling me that *everything* they are doing is important. So I respond by asking, "Why? Tell me why each of these things is so important. What company priority or key value is each item on your agenda linked to? How does each of these items fit within the company's key direction?" I usually get back stares or vague rhetoric. Everything is important, but nothing ties in clearly with the key direction of the company!

Eighty/twenty thinking has to start at the top. If senior management does not set a clear direction for the company by identifying the two or three most important priorities, then the tribes cannot choose their own 20 percent. They have no basis for choosing. Usually they will be forced either to try to do everything or to choose their priorities based on *who* asked them to do a particular task or function. If someone important asks them to do something, then it is top priority. If that "important person" is clear on the company direction, then that item may actually be a top priority. But it is very important to tell the tribes why and how that item is linked to the direction of the company—to not just assume that they understand—if people are going to be able to be committed and focused with their energy.

Jan Carlzon has been successful over the past several years probably because he has managed to communicate a clear and simple set of directions to all the employees at SAS. The key SAS concerns or values of are (1) to provide on-time service to business travelers, and (2) to provide high-quality, responsive customer service. Setting these priorities does not mean that nothing else is important. But it does mean that these two issues are the 20 percent at SAS. These priorities are easy to understand and easy to translate into day-to-day behavior anywhere in the organization. Flowery, eloquent, vague mission statements are not useful to employees in the real world. "Get the planes off on time" is useful—it makes sense. It is a goal, a cause, that employees can rally around.

QUESTIONS TO ASK ABOUT TRIBAL STRESS

Are you having fun at your job? How could you or your tribe make it more fun?

Do some of your personal or tribal values overlap with the organization's values? If you can identify the common ground, you can use it to build personal and tribal commitment.

What are your daydreams about your perfect job or career future? How can you make more of that fantasy happen where you are right now?

What are your biggest work-related fears at this point? Take each of those fears, and describe to yourself what is the most likely, *realistic* outcome of that fear coming true.

What is the worst possible outcome of each of your fears? What is your contingency plan in case that worst-case scenario does happen?

Listen to the "self-talk" chatter that goes on in your head all the time. *Are these thoughts self-abusive?* How would you react if you heard someone saying those words about your best friend? If you would rush to your friend's defense, try rushing to your own defense. Talk to yourself the way you would to your best friend when he or she needs support and encouragement. If you constantly run yourself down by the things you are saying to yourself in your head, it will eventually have the same impact on you as it would if other people were constantly criticizing you.

Thinking of a current problem or project, what are all the control, influence, and "no control" factors you can think of about the situation? Plan your action strategy, or a to-do list, around the control and influence items.

In a recent frustrating situation, can you think of any control or influence factors you overlooked because you were too focused on being frustrated about the "no control" factors?

Listen to the "gripe sessions" in your organization. *How much of the content is focused on "no control" factors?* How could you redirect your contributions to those conversations by focusing on control and influence factors?

Do you have committed people without a cause in your organization? Do people complain regularly about overload? Do they seem to have an agenda of dozens of tasks or projects, all of which are top priority? How do the tribes decide how to use their limited hours, people, dollars, and other resources? Can they clearly state how these resources decisions contribute to the direction of the company?

Do you or your tribe practice 80/20 thinking? *Which of these two statements sounds more like you?* (1) "I give my all to everything I do." (2) "Whatever I do, I do it right, or I don't do it at all." A person can obviously have both attitudes, depending on the circumstances; but which one sounds more like *you?* From my experience in organizations, people who make the first statement often have more problems prioritizing their work, while people who make the second statement are likely to be natural 80/20 types.

What are the key priorities or directions for your organization at this time? Think of two or three tasks, projects, or plans that your tribe is heavily involved in, and see if you can explain in clear and simple terms how those activities fit in with organizational priorities. Of course, if you could not answer the first question, you are going to have a tough time answering the second.

If you have been having a hard time answering these questions about priorities and directions to your satisfaction, try this one. Think of two or three examples of your organization's proudest moments. Those are the events that in your mind symbolize the best that your organization has to offer. These were the times when you were truly proud to be a part of your organization. You may have thought, "If it could be like this all the time, everything would be great here." After you have remembered several of these events, look them over and decide what the common themes are. *What are the values or priorities that these stories represent?* If you end up gleaning values that are too vague—like "quality"—then be more specific. Quality in what? By whose standards? After you come up with a statement or two about key values or priorities, ask yourself whether a front-line employee who had been with the company for two months could understand them. If not, clean them up. Make your statements straightforward and practical. Get rid of fancy language. These statements may not be a complete representation of your company's priorities, but at least they get you in the right ballpark. They will be statements based on real events that you are proud of in your organization.

The changes discussed in this chapter are changes in attitude, or in habitual ways of thinking. These kinds of changes can be made, but it is usually a slow process and takes lots of practice. If a tribe makes a commitment as a group to work on developing attitudes that are more stress-resistant, the members can give each other a great deal of support and encouragement. If you are interested in pursuing this approach in more detail, Kriegel and Kriegel's book, *The C Zone,* and Maddi and Kobasa, *The Hardy Executive,* are excellent sources with many suggestions and practice activities to help you in your efforts.

10 SKILLS FOR MANAGING TRIBES

Managing employees is a complicated and unpredictable task for most people who are promoted into management roles. They have been exceptionally good at the technical or professional skills that go with being a good member of their own tribe, so they are rewarded by being promoted into a position that requires a whole new set of interpersonal and organizational skills. Very few people have a "natural talent" for managing and leading a group of people. They have to learn the skills that go with their new roles, so they take courses and learn from their colleagues how to coach, discipline, delegate, motivate, and so on. Many people who are promoted into management positions work hard at learning these skills and become relatively proficient at the various tasks associated with managing people.

It is possible, however, to learn all the skills needed to be a good manager, but to still not understand the "context" in which they are used. Understanding the tribal characteristics of your organization is a survival skill for managers. Without this understanding, managers see themselves as managing random events and unpredictable personalities. If this were truly the case, managing people would involve a series of individual judgment calls based on intuition or years of accumulated experience and personal wisdom. Needless to say, this would make good management very difficult for most people to accomplish. It would also be very difficult to train people to be managers. You could train them in all the individual skills—coaching, discipline, giving instructions, performance appraisal, and so forth—but how would you train them in when to use certain skills, and in what to specifically say and do? There would be no way to predict every random, unpredictable situation and personality they would encounter.

To address this problem, training often includes the use of examples of typical situations and personalities to teach managers what to say and do in those cases. The hope is that the managers will be able to take the lessons learned from these individual examples and apply them to other circumstances they encounter later. This approach is very helpful, but there is an easier way. If you think about managing people as members of tribes, the situations and personalities become much more predictable. Of course, there are always surprises. But even the surprises usually make more sense if you look at them from a tribal point of view. The roles that a manager must play become clearer as well. It is easier to know at any point in time which role the manager is in, and when he must switch gears into a different role.

As a manager, you are no longer simply a member of your own tribe. Knowing the appropriate internal tribal behavior and the technical skills to do the job is not enough for a manager. As the leader of the tribe, you must now be able to manage the language, values, and rules of the tribe and must ensure that new tribal members are hired who have the appropriate training and thinking abilities for the group. You are also now a member of a new tribe—the management tribe. This is a completely new role, with new language, values, thinking, and rules to consider. When you are promoted into a management position, You are required to give up the one role that is familiar—membership in your own tribe. You then must accept two completely new roles— leader of your own tribe and member of the management tribe. This is a stressful transition under the best of circumstances. If you do not understand these roles or how to use new skills within the new tribal situation, it will be a slower and more difficult transition than necessary.

MANAGER'S ROLES IN A TRIBAL SETTING

From the tribal point of view, there are two roles that a manager plays.

Leader of Your Own Tribe.   In this role, your job is to defend your tribe from outside danger and to manage the tribe's internal functions.

You are, in effect, the keeper of the language, values, training, thinking approaches, and rules. You recruit new tribal members, train them, and keep the ongoing operations functioning as smoothly as possible. Within your tribe there will always be a wide range of individual personalities, but your job is to pull these individuals together and get them to focus on the "situational" personalities that are appropriate for accomplishing your tribe's tasks. As defender of your tribe, your job is to make sure that you have the resources your tribe needs to accomplish its task, campaign for its point of view, and explain your tribal characteristics to other tribes.

Member of the Management Tribe. An equally important role for anyone in a management position is that of management tribe member. In this role, your job is to focus on the umbrella values and quality of the organization and to link the tribes together to enforce these values. When you are in your member role, your own language, values, thinking, and rules may be different from those of your leader role.

Figure 10–1. Balancing Managerial Roles.

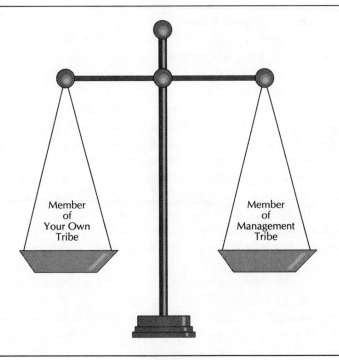

Without the communication skills to migrate and link that were discussed earlier, it is impossible to carry out this role effectively. Migrating and negotiating are the essential skills for management tribe members. Otherwise, all you do is attend management meetings and defend your own tribe. When this happens, you are simply fanning the flames of tribal warfare.

Managers who do not understand the tribal aspects of their organization will often put much more emphasis on their leader role. There are several reasons for this. First of all, they identify much more strongly with their own tribe. They probably were promoted from the ranks of that tribe, and their entire history tells them that this tribe is "home." Secondly, they do not have good migrating and linking skills. Negotiating skills are rarely included in management training. And thirdly, balancing the two roles—tribal leader and management member often feels like walking a tightrope. Shifting back and forth, or doing both roles at once, can be confusing and uncomfortable if you do not understand what the two roles are and how to use them. Both roles are equally important to successful management of people.

Leader of your tribe

Several aspects of the leadership role are discussed in this section to illustrate how to use tribal characteristics to simplify the manager's task and to enhance the quality of the results.

Giving Instructions.   One of the most basic managerial skills within the tribe is the ability to give instructions in a way that produces the results you want. The most useful of the tribal characteristics in this area are thinking patterns. Even though your tribe probably has a general preference for one or two of the thinking patterns, each individual within the tribe will have his own way of thinking. If you do not adjust your instructions to match the receiver's way of thinking, you are not likely to get across the message as you meant it. You say one thing, but the receiver translates that message into his language and hears a very different message. Later, you hear him repeating what you said, or see him doing the task, and react with "That's not what I asked you to do." You may often assume that he either did not listen or is lazy. But he usually feels that he did *exactly* what you said and resents the implication of incompetence. The whole situation ends up being stressful and time-consuming, and the results of the work are rarely satisfactory.

This kind of miscommunication happened a few years ago between a dreamer/machine-gun–thinking manager and a detail-thinking secretary in a small start-up company. Both people were skillful in their jobs and very committed to their tribes. The manager's instructions had to do with a mass mailing that was being prepared. The company did not have a word processor at the time, so the letters were being produced in the old way: by typing the body of the letter, making 200 copies, and then typing in the address and salutation on each copy. The manager had tried to "help" with the project, but quickly lost patience with trying to line up the preprinted *Dear* with the name to be typed in on the same line.

When it came time to do the second mailing, the manager told the secretary, "I've got an idea: leave off the *Dear*. It will be much simpler that way." That is all the manager said. This is a typical dreamer/machine-gun instruction—an end-results idea, communicated in a hurry, with no explanation, and certainly, no procedures spelled out. The secretary looked a little baffled, shook her head, and said, "Okay, if that's what you want." Again, in typical dreamer/machine-gun fashion, the manager did not slow down enough to notice the secretary's hesitancy. So the next week, 200 beautifully typed and formatted letters arrived on the manager's desk—all beginning with, "John," "Tom," "Susan," and so on.

At first, the manager stared at the letters in shock and wondered whether this skillful and loyal secretary was losing her mind. Fortunately, however, the manager had been trained in tribal thinking patterns, and suddenly the words, "Leave off the *Dear*, it will be much simpler that way," came floating back to her. The detail-thinking secretary heard this instruction as a specific procedure and did literally, exactly, what the manager said to do. Later, the manager explained to the secretary that what she had actually meant was: (1) leave off the *Dear* before copying the letters, and then (2) add the *Dear* along with the salutation on each of the 200 letters, "So that you don't have to waste time lining up the name with the preprinted word *Dear*." (Reasons are very important to detail thinkers.)

This is a quick, procedural instruction that makes perfect sense to a detail thinker. The secretary's response to hearing about the mistake was, "I thought that was the *dumbest* thing you've ever told me to do!" They agreed that from then on the secretary should feel free to say

"That sounds dumb," to clarify their communications. But the primary responsibility for the mistake was the manager's. If you are the one trying to communicate—explaining, persuading, or giving instructions—*you* are the one most responsible for migrating and for wording the message in a way that makes sense to the receiver. Blaming the receiver for not listening, being dumb, or having "lost her mind" is rarely accurate and usually damages the relationship between two people.

Notice that this miscommunication was in many ways a typical collision between the manager tribe and the secretary tribe. Any good secretary will always use a lot of detail thinking; it is a primary skill needed for the job. In this case, however, the manager was a business owner who was in a fast-paced, future-oriented gear most of the time. So even though these two people were in the same departmental tribe, their other tribal affiliations collided before they even realized it.

Rewards and Feedback. In performance appraisals and day-to-day feedback, it is important that employees are rewarded for (1) carrying out the tribal functions in a way that conforms to its characteristics, especially its values and definition of quality, and (2) making efforts at cross-tribal communication and negotiation.

Rewards for Carrying Out Internal Tribal Functions. These are rewards for how effectively the employee understands and performs each of the tribal characteristics.

- Does he know the tribal *dialect* and use it appropriately?

- Does his performance contribute to the tribal *values* and to quality?

- Is he adequately *trained* and skillful at his functions within the tribe?

- Does he use the *thinking patterns* that fit with the job, and is he flexible enough to shift gears when necessary to communicate with other people?

- Does he understand the tribal *rules of the game* and play by them?

In carrying out the reward and evaluation process, it is very important that the manager look at the current tribal characteristics to determine whether they are helpful or harmful to the organization. At times, the values or rules within a tribe are destructive to the larger organization. For example, a rule such as, "Tell the customer anything whether it is true or not," is very likely to be damaging to the organization. Instead of rewarding employees for carrying out this rule as it is, the manager needs to work toward changing it. It would not make sense to see written on an employee's performance appraisal, as positive feedback "Lies well to the customer."

In describing the tribal characteristics earlier in this book, I did not attempt to evaluate which were positive or negative. That kind of evaluation is the responsibility of the managers of tribes. Ultimately, the customers and the public will give their opinions of your tribal behavior. If they do not agree with you, they have a powerful solution to the problem—they put you out of business.

Rewards for Efforts at Cross-tribal Communication.   Although the manager has more opportunity to migrate and negotiate with other tribes in the organization, the front-line employees can usually play a part in negotiating peaceful settlements with other tribes. If they are skillful at doing this, the manager often does not have to get involved in potential warfare situations. Conflicts are settled by the people closest to the action; they usually know the best solutions anyway. It is important that tribal members be rewarded—verbally, and in writing—for their cross-tribal successes. If the manager pays attention to their efforts to migrate and negotiate with other tribes and includes it in their performance appraisals, the members of the tribe will be getting the clear message that such efforts are important and worth repeating.

Hiring, Firing and Promoting.   There are two tribal skills to look for when hiring or promoting personnel.

Fitting into the tribe.   The person needs to be willing to not only learn the technical functions of the job but to conform to the tribe's characteristics. This necessity can be seen in the health care industry; because of increased competition, many hospitals have become much more concerned in recent years about positive customer relations and image in the community. These hospitals have added a new value— that quality is satisfied patients—and a new rule, "The patient comes first." These new characteristics have had an impact on hiring and promotion. It used to make sense to hire nurses, lab techs, or business office clerks strictly for their technical skills. Now they must have the technical skills plus either good interpersonal skills or the willingness to learn them.

The same considerations affect the firing of an employee. An employee can be a good technician, but may violate the tribal rules around teamwork, honesty, or other interpersonal issues. If the employee is not willing to learn and adapt to the tribal expectation, there are times when their termination is the only choice that is in the tribal and organizational best interest. There are, of course, specific legal guidelines to follow when terminating an employee for these or any other reasons.

Flexibility and willingness to share responsibility for cross-tribal negotiation. One way to think about this issue is to ask the question, how territorial is this person? A new hire is often hard to evaluate on this. Often, you have to base your assessment on the comments of references and on the range of experiences the person has had.

I would suggest that you develop some open-ended, "What would you do if . . . ?" questions for your interviews, so that the potential employee can describe how he would handle cross-tribal situations. These questions and answers are only hypothetical, but they may give you some clues about a person's flexibility and current level of migrating skills. Do not, however, underestimate a person's ability to learn. If you believe in the employees and provide good training and support, people can do amazing things. The self-fulfilling prophecy—you often get from people exactly what you expect from them-actually does work in many cases.

Member of the Management Tribe

The responsibilities that go with the member role have the purpose of building and protecting relationships with other tribes. The management tribe also has the primary responsibility for the umbrella values or mission of the organization.

Management Meetings. In many organizations, managers, meetings or one-on-one encounters between managers are used mainly to do battle or to defend turf. Winning a round with another department means that you did not lose any of your own tribal turf—or even better, you managed to take some turf away from the other tribe. *Turf* usually translates as some resource, such as space, budget dollars, personnel, time, and so forth.

When managers see themselves only as leaders of their own tribe and ignore their role as a member of the management team, they fight for all the resources or turf they can get and then hoard it carefully once they get it. When managers are focused on their management member role, they will emphasize migrating and linking the tribes together. Each manager will, of course, still present his own tribe's point of view, but he will also consider the other tribe's comments and look for ways to link the two together.

During these kinds of negotiations, managers are likely to feel that they are walking a tightrope, trying to balance the leader and member roles. To carry out his management responsibility effectively, the manager has to walk that tightrope. If he gives up and chooses to go with only one role or the other, the solutions that he negotiates will not be as good as they could have been. Either the tribe or the organization is likely to get shortchanged.

Relationships With Outside Tribes.   All the members of the management tribe have some responsibility for managing the relationships with tribes outside the organization—with customers, vendors, the public, and other industries. This is not just the responsibility of the sales or public relations tribes. Each organization will have different outside tribes that are important to them. For some organizations the individual retail customers are the most important outside tribe. For a manufacturing company that produces steel, the industries that buy its product will be its most important outside tribes. Nonprofit associations may emphasize the donors or the public.

An important management task is to know who your most important outside tribes are and to be sure that all members of the team have some regular contact with them. Otherwise, some of the tribes will know and understand those important outsiders, and others will not. If the leaders of some of the tribes do not know the important outside tribes, the ability of the management team to negotiate in the best interests of the outside tribes will be severely limited.

LEARNING TO BE A MANAGER

A manager who has been a member of several tribes before being promoted into management is more likely to see the organization in a flexible way. If, on the other hand, a manager has always been in one department or speciality, his perspective is likely to be narrower, making it harder for him to be flexible and generate alternative solutions that will meet the needs of a number of the tribes.

Lateral moves early in your career, particularly in the lower rungs of management, are helpful in making you a good management team member. You are more likely to truly understand the umbrella values of your organization, not just your own tribal values. There are, of course, people who have not made lateral moves throughout the company who still manage to acquire a broad perspective. They seem to have a natural curiosity and manage to learn how the organization functions from many angles. Even these people, however, could probably know more and understand more clearly how the various tribes function if they had made a few lateral moves around the organization.

Managers who learn to look at the whole organization and who examine how all the parts fit together to accomplish the overall mission not only make good members of the management tribe but also are better leaders of their own tribes. They develop an understanding for what I call the "ripple effect" of management decisions—all the other behaviors and attitudes that are affected because of one management action.

Many of these behavior effects may be unintentional, but at times they can be very negative. For example, if you fire one employee in a tribe and fail to communicate clearly to all the other tribal members why and how that happened, you have to deal with all kinds of secondary effects from that decision. The other employees guess at the reasons for the firing, they may be less likely to trust the manager enough to share any failures because it might mean the end for them, too, or they may even request transfers out of the department or start job-hunting. On the other hand, if the firing is handled in a clear-cut, fair way and reasons for it are communicated to the employees in a way that enables them to understand the implications for their own behavior, then the manager can end up a hero. When a manager not only fires an employee who everyone in the tribe knew needed to leave, but does it in a humane way, the respect for that leader usually skyrockets.

Many times a tribe comes up with a great idea, but forgets that other tribes need to be involved. Halfway through the implementation of the great idea, several other tribes get wind of what is going on and have a fit. Many innovations in organizations are stopped dead in their tracks because the managers did not know how to implement a great idea by thinking it through from a systems point of view and considering the ripple effect.

MANAGING THE MANAGERS

In multitiered organizations, there are one or more layers of upper level managers who are responsible for managing divisions that consist of a number of departments. A division head is not simply the leader of one tribe; he is the leader of a cluster of tribes, and he is primarily focused on coordination of their efforts to keep them all linked to the rest of the organization. This is often a more complex role than a department-level manager's job. People who have been very skillful as leaders of their own tribes can have a difficult time adjusting to this new and expanded role after they are promoted. Their loyalties may stay with their original "home" tribe, making it easy for them to see only that point of view in any dispute or planning effort. Or they may know they need to broaden their perspective, but also know that it takes the time and effort to learn enough about the other areas to be able to truly see the "big picture."

One variable that can make a great deal of difference in how easily a manager makes this transition has to do with the historical level of tribal warfare. In an organization that consistently encourages its tribes to look at the big picture and to focus on umbrella values as a basis for decisions and negotiation, the newly promoted division head will be fairly well trained in the leadership thinking that is needed to carry out these responsibilities. But in an organization that stresses loyalty to your own tribe and high levels of turf protection, the new division head may not even have a clear understanding of the focus and priorities of the organization, let alone the skills for leading a complex cluster of tribes in the right directions for carrying out those priorities.

Division heads and senior managers have three main responsibilities in leading the organization's tribes:

1. Participating in the development and constant refinement of the organization's umbrella values
2. Communicating the big picture to the tribes within their division, and guiding decisions and behaviors in directions that will make the organization successful in carrying out the umbrella values
3. Linking the tribes in the division with all other areas of the company in a way that fosters innovative, productive solutions

It would be difficult to prioritize these three responsibilities; all of them are essential aspects of a well-coordinated organization. Covering these three areas well, along with all the other responsibilities that come with a senior manager's role, is an overwhelming task. It is probably essential that a manager be capable of applying the 80/20 mode of thinking when prioritizing the most important aspects of these responsibilities. For each one, the senior manager must ask the question, "What 20 percent of my activities in this area will give me 80 percent of my results?" Concentrating time and energy on the 20-percent will usually be enough to produce good results.

What are senior management's 20-percent priorities in each of the three responsibilities described above? There is, of course, no single answer to that question, depending as it does on circumstances. But there are at least a few general guidelines to consider when setting your own 20-percent priorities.

There are often two very important elements in developing and refining the company's umbrella values. One is spending enough time with your customer or constituency to know what they are thinking and what they need from your organization. The second is knowing who the people with influence are in your organization, and then spending your time communicating with them and selling them on your ideas for the company.

The most important 20-percent priority in communicating umbrella values to your division's tribes is likely to be the skill of delegating and inspiring your next tier of managers. The rule of thumb for senior management needs to be: Educate your managers, inspire them, and then get out of their way and let them go do it. The front-line employees also need to hear directly from you at times, but this kind of communication is not as likely to be a 20-percent priority, as is the skill of delegating and creating good leadership below you.

In the third area of responsibility, modeling skillful migrating and negotiating behavior may be one of the most important things you can do to create linkages between divisions and to demonstrate that you are serious about collaboration within the company. In the same vein, rewarding the people in your division for their own efforts at linkage is worth considering as a 20-percent priority.

Senior management of an organization sets the tone and the expectations for warfare or for peace. The top people in organizations often express amazement at the level of attention that is paid within the organization to their every move. My advice is to get used to it! The tribes are indeed watching every move you make, and for the most part, will model their own behavior after what they see coming from you. Warfare at the top or fuzzy priorities will have a ripple effect down through the organization and will produce turf protection, not teamwork.

QUESTIONS TO ASK ABOUT MANAGING TRIBES

Do your managers seem to clearly understand that they are both the leader of their own tribe and a member of the management tribe? Look at their behavior when they are in meetings, or working together on a problem one on one. If they understand both roles, they will be simultaneously skillful at defending their own tribe's point of view and at negotiating solutions that are good for the organization.

If you are the leader of your tribe, you are the "keeper" of the tribal characteristics—especially the values and rules. *Are your tribal values and rules good for the tribe and the company?* Do your tribal values fit easily under your organization's umbrella values? Are the members of your tribe rewarded for good tribal behavior and for good intertribal negotiation? Does your tribe tell stories that reflect a "We showed them!" attitude toward other tribes? If so, you are probably too territorial. It is dangerous when the perceived enemy is within the organization. "We showed them!" is fine if it is applied to the competition, but destructive if it denotes tribal warfare in the organization.

In management meetings or in one-on-one encounters, do managers focus on migrating and linking between the tribes? Defending your own tribe is one role you play in negotiations, but everyone's attitude and tone should emphasize the linkage between tribal points of view, as well as solutions that are best for the organization. Is migrating the expected, normal behavior between managers in your organization?

Do all members of the management tribe play some role in developing relationships with tribes outside your organization—with customers, vendors, the public, and others? In most organizations, some of the umbrella values relate to the way those outside groups are treated. If managers have no role in creating and protecting those relationships, it is unlikely that their tribes will feel any real responsibility for carrying out those values. If customers, for example, are an abstract idea to a tribe, rather than real people they, "Who cares" rules are very likely to develop in that tribe.

Does your organization encourage lateral moves of employees from one tribe to another? This is a good way to cross-fertilize the tribes and keep their perspectives a little more flexible. After employees have made such moves, they will retain their old tribal "memory" for a period of time, but eventually they will forget and will become completely absorbed in the new tribe's point of view. It is necessary for lateral moves to be a common occurrence in an organization if it is to get as much mileage out of this strategy as possible.

Does your leadership training for managers focus on the whole organization and teach them how all the parts fit together? Are negotiation skills stressed in the training? Is the tone of the training turf-oriented or not?

If you are a manager, are you willing to walk the tightrope between the leader and member roles? Can you think of times when you have done a good job of balancing the two roles? Many managers are very willing to play the leader role, but are not too excited about the member role. I often tell groups of managers that one of the main things they are paid higher salaries for is that tightrope. If they had the luxury of doing only one role or the other, their jobs would be relatively easy. But the fact is that they do not have that choice. If they choose to fill only one of those roles, then they are not doing the job that the organization hired them to do.

If you are a senior manager and have a number of different tribes reporting to you what are your priorities in the following three key responsibilities in managing tribes from the top? What is the 20 percent of your efforts in each of these areas that is likely to produce 80 percent of your results?

1. Participating in the development and constant refinement of the umbrella values for the organization as a whole.
2. Communicating this big picture perspective to the tribes within your division and guiding decisions and behaviors in directions that will help the organization succeed in carrying out these values.
3. Linking the tribes in the division with all the other areas of the company in a way that fosters innovative, productive solutions.

All three responsibilities are essential aspects of leading the tribes in your organization toward more teamwork and less turf protection. It is important that senior managers have some strategies in mind for accomplishing these goals.

11 INNOVATION
Cross-tribal Fertilization

Almost every industry and business is caught up in the current whirl-wind of rapid change. Products change, services expand, regulations increase and decrease—these are just some of the changes that have been triggered by the shift away from an industrial-based economy toward a service economy. Under these circumstances, constant innovation is a survival strategy for businesses. An organization must keep coming up with new ideas to expand and streamline its operations just to keep even with the market and its competition, let alone to be a front-runner or pace-setter for its industry or profession.

One of the key elements that will determine whether or not an organization is successful at implementing innovation is the quality of communication between its tribes. If you define *innovation* as new ideas that are put to practical use within an organization, you can quickly see that more than one tribe will almost always be needed to successfully innovate. New ideas rarely fit neatly within the turf of only one tribe. Implementing a new service or product takes the efforts of the design, production, marketing, and accounting tribes. A new approach to inventory control will affect every tribe in the organization in one way or another. When these kinds of changes affect more than one group, there will be a need for negotiation and joint efforts between the tribes.

The ability and willingness to migrate will be essential to ensure that new ideas do not die on the vine. If your organization has a history of tribal warfare, however, you are likely to have a battle over every square inch of tribal turf. Anything that concerns staffing, scheduling, budget, supplies, time, or any other tribal resource will be seen as a threat. If you look at innovation and new ideas from only one tribe's point of view, these ideas are usually dangerous invasions that need to be stopped. If, on the other hand, several tribes are able to work together on figuring out how to implement these same ideas, the benefits of change are much clearer. It will also be more likely that you can implement change in a way that protects each of the tribes as much as possible. In short, an organization with a history of serious tribal warfare will find it almost impossible to innovate effectively.

BETTER WAYS OF DOING
WHAT YOU ALREADY DO

Innovation is often seen in organizations as a totally new set of activities that will cost money, take time, and put further stress and demands on an already overburdened staff. Many businesses are wary of committing themselves to "becoming more innovative" because they see this as synonymous with a new drain on resources. Many of the workshops on creativity only serve to confirm their worst fears. Often, the purpose of these workshops is to encourage free-wheeling thinking and wild ideas for the future of the organization. Most of these ideas would, of course, cost large sums of money. These kinds of workshops have a serious organizational side effect—they give the finance tribe ulcers! There is nothing wrong with creative, future-oriented thinking, as long as it can be turned into practical ideas that can be used by the organization. Many new ideas for products and services are generated this way.

There is, however, another way of approaching innovation that may be even more useful to organizations on a day-to-day basis. In this approach, innovation itself becomes a background issue; "innovative" refers to the *way* you do the things that you are already going to be doing anyway. The emphasis is not on new products and services but on operations. Ideas are analyzed not just for what they will cost, but for what they will save. This approach to innovation is not so ulcer-producing for the finance tribe and is usually easier to implement for any organization that is in a period of financial hard times or cost constraint.

These two approaches to innovation are, in effect, two different definitions of innovation. Depending on which approach you emphasize, the implications for tribal behavior will be different. The terms resourceful and original are often used to describe these two approaches to innovation.[1] Resourceful thinking tends to stay within the current boundaries of a situation and to look for ways to improve the status quo. Original thinking, on the other hand, goes outside the current boundaries and redefines the basic problem itself. It is the less structured and more creative approach.

In general, resourceful thinking is more useful at the mature stages of a product life cycle, for dealing with short-term concerns, or for small-budget projects. Original thinking is better suited to serious crisis situations, large budgets, long-term projects, or problems that recur over and over, no matter how many efforts are made to improve or fix them.

An organization could emphasize one or the other of these approaches at different times depending on the circumstances. There are skills associated with each approach, and most tribes usually have a natural talent for one or the other kind of thinking. Knowing that both approaches exist will help you tap your organization's range of innovative talents as needed.

"DREAMERS WHO DO": SKILLS FOR INNOVATING

"Dreamers who do" is the phrase coined by Gifford Pinchot, to describe the few people in every tribe who are skillful at both dreaming and doing and who are well-rounded, all-purpose innovators.[3] There are many more people in every tribe who are skillful at *either* dreaming or doing, but not necessarily at both. Those who can do both are excellent resources for making innovation happen. But you can pull together teams of dreamers and doers and teach them how to function as effectively as individual innovators.

Although there are dreamers, doers, and "dreamers who do" in most tribes, they are not always evenly distributed. Some tribes attract dreamers—strategic planning, marketing, research and development, internal consulting. Other tribes are more likely to attract doers—technical services, production, accounting, quality control. These differences can be valuable in creating innovative teams, or they can be the source of tribal warfare. Dreamers and doers usually find each other very irritating. But if they are trained in migrating and in blending their talents, you can have high-quality innovation as well as rewarding experiences for all concerned. "Dreamers who do" are often the best leaders for these teams. They are able to demonstrate to the team members that there is value in all of their perspectives and skills.

By having a balance of dreamers and doers on your innovation teams, you are more likely to have a balance between ideas and facts when your teams are working on development of new products or procedures for the company. The doers will concentrate on the facts of the situation, researching and gathering the data needed to make informed decisions. The dreamers, on the other hand, will be more likely to keep new ideas flowing, building on the original idea. This talent can be very helpful when the team runs into unforeseen roadblocks that threaten the project. A continual flow of new ideas balanced by data and facts supporting all decisions is the ideal combination for an innovation team. It takes both dreamers and doers to have this balance—a few "dreamers who do" are probably also required to keep the peace between them.

This combination is critical in companies that rely heavily on the work of scientists to produce its products and services. Unfortunately, there is often a great deal of conflict between the scientists and the business managers in a company. Management is naturally interested in quick, low-cost production of a marketable product. In other words, managers are interested in "applied" research. The scientists, on the other hand, often have difficulty convincing management that "basic" research is an important aspect of their work. From the scientists' perspective, their work cannot be subjected to the same kinds of cost-effectiveness measures and manufacturing standards that are used for the production departments.[4] This is a classic case of a collision between two very different tribes.

According to Harvey Sherman, a former president of the American Society for Public Administration, "The industrial executive sees the scientist as a narrow specialist with no interest in efficiency or economy, or in the overall objectives of the enterprise; a person who . . .objects to all types of control, and who is more interested in impressing other members of his profession than in the success of the enterprise for which he works." The scientist takes an equally unflattering view of the executive. "The scientist sees him as a bureaucrat, a paper shuffler, a parasite, an uncreative and unoriginal hack who serves as an obstacle in the way of creative people trying to do a job, and a person more interested in dollars and power than in knowledge and innovation."[5] In this scenario, the dreamers and the doers are in conflict. Ideas and facts are both essential to produce the products that drive the science-based industries, but a meeting of the minds between these two tribes is a constant struggle.

CROSS-TRIBAL INNOVATION TEAMS

There are several considerations to keep in mind when organizing cross-tribal teams for innovation.

1. *Be sure you have a mixture of dreamers, doers and "dreamers who do."* To determine who these people are in your organization, use the information on thinking patterns in Chapter 6 as a guide. People who rate their mode of thinking as "dreamer" tend to be the dreamers as Pinchot defines them. People who rate themselves dominant in detail thinking tend to be the doers. People who rate their thinking as a mixture of several modes are more likely to be the "dreamers who do."

Use the checklist in the questions at the end of Chapter 6. Be sure you have a mixture of dreamers, doers, and "dreamers who do" on your innovation team. A team of all dreamers will have great ideas, but will probably never implement anything. A team of doers will develop great implementation plans and budgets for outdated ideas. A group with no "dreamers who do" will have a leadership or diplomacy gap—no one to help the team members work together or to keep them communicating. If you do not have these well-rounded innovators within your organization, use outsiders. But do not be too quick to assume that there are no natural innovators in your organization. In any organization, there are "closet" innovators who are hidden because no one has ever gone looking for them. In the past, acting like an innovator was a well-known CSG, (Career-Shortening Gesture) in most organizations. Often the best way to identify these closet innovators is to ask for volunteers to participate in developing some new product or service. This is when they often step forward.

2. *Be sure that the tribes who will be affected by the innovation are represented on the team.* If you are implementing a big change that will affect many tribes, you may need several teams to work on various aspects of the change. Or you can have related tribes all represented by one member of the team. Some teams are set up to have at least one rotating slot that is filled by one tribal representative for a few weeks or months and then rotates to someone else from another tribe. Leaving

out some tribes because you "don't have the time" or "it's too much trouble" is usually a set-up for worse trouble later. If a tribe was not a part of the planning, it will take no ownership in the new idea and has very little reason to care whether it succeeds or not.

3. *Focus on the organization's umbrella values.* The new product, service, or operations idea that the team works on will have more meaning if it is clearly connected to at least one umbrella value. These values give the team members a basis for migrating and for negotiating the differences between the tribal points of view they represent. Umbrella values remind them that here is a larger mission they are all a part of in creating the new innovation.

4. *Soliciting voluntary membership on innovation teams is usually the best way to go.* You will attract the people who have the most interest in the new idea, as well as your most committed dreamers and doers. Realistically, however, volunteers are usually "persuaded." Getting the variety of participants needed for these teams usually requires some recruiting efforts, such as invitations from senior management or nomination by the departmental tribe. But at least make an effort to avoid forced participation. Coercion into innovation rarely works.

5. *Be sure there are rewards for participating in these cross-tribal teams.* Migrating out of your own tribe takes effort and is not always a comfortable experience, even if it is only temporary. There needs to be some concrete payoff for doing it. Meaningful rewards for participating in cross-tribal teams are the best ways to let everyone in the organization know that this is valued behavior, and worth the effort.

Pinchot tells a wonderful story about the method that one of his "intrapreneurs" used to find engineers for his innovation teams.[6] He made four lists of potential candidates. First, he went to Personnel and got a list of all the people who were "good engineers, but. . . ." He did not care what the "but" was in reference to, although it usually indicated that the person was some kind of troublemaker. Then, he went to the model shop and asked the machinists which engineers knew what they were doing in a hands-on way. Next, he went out to the parking lot and took down the license plate numbers of all the motorcycles and pick-up trucks then cross-referenced these numbers with the company roster to find out which ones belonged to engineers. Finally, he found out which engineers were skydivers, rock climbers, or hang gliders. If an engineer's name appeared on two or more lists, he knew he had identified a serious maverick—and a good candidate for his innovation team.

BUILDING ON STRENGTHS

Peter Drucker, the well-known American management expert, has been famous for years for encouraging businesses to spend more time and energy building on their strengths. According to Drucker, successful innovators look for opportunities that "fit me, fit this company, put to work what we are good at and have shown capacity for in performance."[7] He stresses, for example, that a business needs to be sure that there is a "fit" between the new idea for a product and the company. Businesses rarely do well with a product that does not match their other product lines in some way. He cites a pharmaceutical company trying to do well in something as "frivolous" as lipsticks or perfumes.[8] Innovation takes a great deal of hard work, persistence, and dedication all of which are more likely to occur if the new ideas build on the strengths that already exist in the organization.

Individuals in organizations are often so focused on the daily problems to be solved and on the downside of events that they end up ignoring the upside potential and other possibilities all around them. I have often asked groups of employees to list the strengths and problems within their department or organization. Without exception, in every organization where I have used this exercise, the problems list is longer than the strengths list. I do not believe that this gives an accurate picture of most of these organizations. I think it is a habit of thinking that causes most of us to pay attention mostly to problems.

This habit of focusing on the negative is a dangerous impediment to innovation. Most new ideas come from thinking about possibilities and about an open-ended future. Putting out fires and solving problems do not tend to trigger interesting, new ideas.

Another danger with this kind of negative thinking is that you will not take advantage of the talents and skills that are available within your tribes. Talents are ignored, or even seen as problems. 3M Corporation is widely considered to be one of the most innovative companies in the world. One of their senior vice presidents spoke to a group of health care executives who were interested in fostering more innovation. He warned these CEOs to be prepared for the irritating characteristics of their in-house innovators. He said he often found himself driving home from work at the end of a particularly frustrating day in a terrible mood, with a splitting headache, because of one of those damned innovators. Even as the audience laughed and nodded, he was quick to point out that the problems were well worth suffering through because the strengths of these innovators were the backbone of 3M's success.

NEGATIVE CORPORATE POLITICS

Corporate politics is a term that usually carries the negative connotation of plotting and scheming to promote yourself, your career, or your own ideas, whether or not it is in your company's best interest to do so. There are, of course, some political skills that are productive for your company and essential for anyone who works in a large, complex organization. Negative corporate politics, however, are the death of innovation in any company. People spend their time tracking the latest political moves and constantly keeping up with the newest buzzwords and themes so that they can position themselves for a promotion or to take credit for some piece of the latest trend. Taking risks for a good idea or sticking your neck out to support an individual or team wanting to try something controversial is considered foolhardy in this environment.

Do not misunderstand—there is still a great deal of *talk* about innovation, risk, and daring new ideas in a company riddled with negative politics. It is just that no one *does* anything that is particularly innovative, risk-taking, or daring. If someone does try to make an innovative effort, that person better be certain of success. Failure at any major efforts in a political company can be fatal to one's image. If you do fail, it is very important that you bury it as quickly as possible, so that no one knows about it.

Fear commonly goes with negative politics. Employees at all levels are afraid of ever being seen in a bad light because image and positioning are essential to their success. Cynicism is another feeling common to highly political environments. People do not believe that anyone is telling the truth or that anyone will really be rewarded for characteristics such as courage and risk-taking for the good of the company.

In one highly political corporation that had the companywide rule of the game, say what is expedient instead of the truth, any exception was a rare event worth noting. A front-line employee of the company was having a casual conversation with a manager from her division who had recently left the company. This employee had not known the manager very well, but told him that she had always remembered him as the only person who had ever walked into her office and "just told me the truth like that was normal behavior around here!" The ex-manager laughed and explained that he had always known he was playing against the unspoken rules, but had decided to play dumb and push the truth as far as it could go. Needless to say, he had eventually decided that it was better to move on to a more innovative and less political company to continue his career growth.

QUESTIONS TO ASK ABOUT INNOVATION AND YOUR TRIBES

Is your organization geared toward resourceful thinking or toward original thinking in its approach to innovation? Can you think of times when one or the other approach would have been more appropriate because of the kind of problem being addressed? Think of several recent "new ideas" in your organization. Were they ideas that would have improved and streamlined operations, or were they ideas for doing things in a completely different way?

Identify the dreamer tribes and the doer tribes in your organization. *Which tribes are a mixture of both?* List the two or three main functions of several of the tribes in your organization. Then look over each list and decide if those functions are likely to be done by dreamers or doers or by a combination of the two. This will give you some indication of the style of each tribe. There may, of course, be many individuals in a tribe who do not match the tribal pattern. But the tribe usually does have a group pattern, and this pattern usually matches their key functions.

Who are the "dreamers who do" in your organization? If you cannot think of anyone, do not be too quick to assume that they do not exist. They are probably in hiding. If there is no clear history in your organization of rewarding innovators and valuing people who are good at dreaming up new ideas and making them happen, then these people are more likely to do their innovating at home, where the risks are less and the rewards are at least personally satisfying. As you get started in your innovation efforts, these people will gradually surface.

What are the talents that the tribes in your company could bring to the table in an innovation effort? Some of these talents will be the expertise of the tribe, such as the finance tribe's ability to run the numbers and figure the cost-effectiveness of new ideas. Other talents will be more personal, belonging to certain individuals within the tribes.

What are some meaningful rewards that could be used in your organization to recognize efforts at cross-tribal innovation? Often the best source of ideas for rewards is the employees themselves. If you do not have money to offer, tell them so. Ask them for nonmonetary ideas. Employees are often very innovative when it comes to dreaming up rewards.

It may still be worth considering monetary rewards whenever possible. Many companies are adopting policies that enable employees who develop a new idea that produces money for the company to share in the profits on a percentage basis for a certain period of time. Companies may be too quick to assume that they do not have money to offer, overlooking the possibility of sharing future returns rather than current available dollars.

The most important part of the process of cross-tribal innovation is simply getting started. Pull some teams together and let the cross-fertilization of ideas begin. Many organizations are intimidated by the idea of trying to become more innovative. They think that they need a multimillion-dollar budget, new employees, and extensive training before they can start. But one of the basic rules of innovation is *think small*. Get started on a small scale and use your tribal talents.

12 ORGANIZATIONAL STRUCTURES AND TRIBAL WARFARE

Most of this book has been devoted to "people" strategies for reducing tribal warfare in organizations. Understanding the differences between tribes and knowing how to negotiate these differences are communication skills that individuals and departments can learn. This chapter will look at a different set of strategies that can also help to reduce conflict between tribes. These strategies involve the structure and environment of the company, everything from the design of a new building to the rankings on the organizational chart.

These structural strategies set the stage or the atmosphere within which people work. If structures are handled in a way that increases positive contact between tribes, it is easier for employees to use their communication skills to negotiate and work together effectively. Structural strategies, however, are never a substitute for the "people" strategies. You can have an ideally designed layout and operation for your facility, but it will be of no help at all in reducing conflict unless the employees have the personal skills to make this structure work for them.

My purpose is not necessarily to suggest major, sweeping changes in your organization. It is rarely possible, for example, to tear down the building and start all over. The purpose is to sensitize you to the many opportunities—small and large—to keep your organization moving in the direction of positive contact between the tribes and efforts toward greater harmony.

Most of the structural mistakes made by organizations are accidental, often done with the best of intentions. I saw one large corporation build a new office building for one of its divisions. To the delight of its employees, the building was designed with all its offices having permanent walls and doors—no more cubicles and cubbyholes! The old building was abandoned with glee. But within a month of moving into the new building, "alienation" set in. People started commenting on the fact that they never saw each other any more. More meetings had to be scheduled to keep everyone up-to-date. More memos and paper started to circulate. The teamwork of that division never returned to its "old-building" levels, and in fact the division no longer exists at all. The new building, of course, was only one factor influencing the demise of the division, but it did play a role in the loss of productivity and morale.

I saw another company move from an old, outdated building with many of the same drawbacks. The employees of this company were also pleased to be moving to a brand-new building designed just for them. Each floor of this building was almost all glass—offices, some conference rooms, the center staircase connecting all floors. This company built a much larger lunchroom than it had had before. The elevators were wall-to-wall mirrors and an intercom reached all floors. People regularly comment that they now know other employees who they had never seen before, or did not even realize worked for the same company. An unexpected by-product—less tribal warfare.

THE PHYSICAL PLANT

One of the most important structures that has an impact on employees is the building itself. If you happen to be planning a new building, you have a great opportunity to design the structure to address tribal issues. Architects are often unaware of these concerns. The people who work in the company are the ones who will know which tribes need to have more contact and what kind of layout would produce positive results. No two companies are exactly alike.

One tribal issue that I run into repeatedly is what I have started calling the "upstairs-downstairs syndrome." It is easiest to see in a small company that is housed in a two-story building with personnel divided between the first and second floors. For some reason, senior management—or at least the CEO—is usually upstairs. Everyone else is clustered by tribe and located on one floor or the other. There is far more contact between tribes that work on the same floor of the building. All the tribes on the other floor fall clearly into the category of "those other guys." In a larger organization, it gets even more complicated, with more floors and different buildings influencing tribal relationships.

I sometimes listen to the upstairs-downstairs stories from various employees and conclude that we would all be better off if companies would build only one story buildings! That, of course, is not a realistic solution to this problem, but there are a few strategies that I have seen organizations use that do seem to help.

In a small organization, it may be possible to mix the tribes on each floor. It may not actually be necessary to have everyone from one tribe clustered together on one floor. This strategy will often be unworkable because of each tribe's need for contact among themselves or because of equipment and systems constraints. But it is at least a possibility worth considering.

Another strategy that I was personally a part of in a large corporation was moving people around frequently to break down the "my building-your building" attitude. During my five-year tenure at that company, I worked in seven different offices in six different buildings. I used to laugh and claim that my best corporate skill was moving! Although it was a pain in the neck at times, one of the positive by-products of this constant flux was feeling "at home" in every building the company owned. I knew people everywhere I went. I knew where to find all the vending machines, bathrooms, drinking fountains, supply rooms, copy machines. I even knew where to find the hidden parking spots in the crowded lots outside each building. In other words, I did not feel like I was on alien turf anywhere I went in that company. I never got too attached to one office or building because I knew I probably would not be there long. So, rather than identifying with one building, floor, or group of people, I identified with the company.

It is more difficult to launch a tribal war with a person who used to work in the next office and shared a kitchenette with you. And even if you do get into it with each other at times, you both have your past relationship to protect, so you are a little more willing to negotiate.

Another area of office buildings that I am always interested is what I call the watering holes—break rooms, lunchrooms, and other hangout spots. A new one in many buildings these days is outside on the sidewalk by the entrance. This one is being used even in the dead of winter in some companies because of the new no-smoking policies coming into effect everywhere. I know when there is a no-smoking policy at a client company even before I walk through the front door for the first time. At any time of day, there are at least two or three people standing around the front door, puffing away. The policy has inadvertently created a new watering hole. Considering the impression made on visitors and customers, the front door of the building may not be the ideal spot for this to occur. But unless another spot is provided or mandated, this is where employees seem to naturally end up.

It is useful to know who uses these watering holes. The cafeteria, for example, usually attracts large percentages of certain tribes. If employees from many different groups do use the cafeteria, then often you find that they only sit with their own tribes. In one company, I was told that operations personnel and the sales force never sat together. The break room had two tables that would each seat several people. A member of the sales tribe told me that if she walked in to get a snack and there were several operations people sitting together at one table with one leftover chair, she would never go and sit with them. She said that, in the first place they were probably talking about either her or one of her tribal members. And in the second place, she did not want to sit with them anyway. If other sales members of her tribe walked through, it would "look funny" for her to be sitting with operations people. This in itself is not tribal warfare, but the stage for trouble between these two groups has been set in their break room.

Elevators and parking lots are also an interesting study in tribal behavior. In some companies the elevators serve as spots for a quick, friendly party of sorts; but in other companies the rule of the game is to stare straight ahead and mind your own business. If anyone talks at all, it's in a whisper. Mirrors in elevators will often force people to talk a little more. Sometimes the conversation level in elevators seems to be regulated by who steps on and off during the ride. Certain tribes may chat openly with each other, but when the door opens and "someone else" steps on, silence descends. Three floors later the unwelcome or intimidating person steps off, and the conversation picks up where it left off. Usually the tribal membership rather than the known personality of the offending person triggers this reaction.

During a session on customer relations training for a company, I was haranguing the group about elevator behavior and its impact on customers. Several of the front-line employees came up afterwards to tell me that the "blue suits" were the ones who needed to listen to that message. According to these people, the "'blue suits" only talk to each other on elevators, and when they get on, everyone else quits talking completely. You probably will not be surprised to hear that this particular organization is one of the most skillful at guerrilla warfare tactics of any I have seen. There is more than one way to get a "blue suit"!

TOO MANY LAYERS, TOO MANY TRIBES

If your organization has become a hierarchical, many-tiered bureaucracy, then you may simply have too many tribes. Chances are, some of your departments have practically nothing to do with directly carrying out the organization's umbrella values and current priorities. There are probably also too many layers of management tribes.

If you are trying to minimize tribal warfare in your organization, you will obviously be better off if you do not have any more tribes than necessary. One danger from tribes that are not really central to the values and priorities of an organization is that they sense that they are expendable, become justifiably paranoid, and fight even harder for their own turf and survival. They cannot afford to be focused on and committed to the organization's larger needs. They are fighting not only for their own tribal survival but probably for each tribal member's job security.

One common statement made about American businesses is that most of them could cut 25 percent of their work force and not be substantially hurt in their ability to produce quality products and services. I seriously doubt that this statistic is accurate. I think most organizations need a more labor-intensive work force to produce the *customer's* definition of quality than the productivity experts realize. But some organizations with cumbersome bureaucracies may need to look hard at the issue of too many tribes.

One of the most common reasons that an organization has too many tribes is changes in their industry or company. A tribe that was vital five years ago may be outmoded and unnecessary today. But the company is hesitant to disband the department or division, either for public relations reasons or out of concern for the employees whose jobs would be affected. Although these reasons are understandable, there still must be a better solution than retaining departments and functions that are no longer relevant to the company's ability to carry out its mission. Phaseouts, attrition, and relocation of employees are strategies that can be used. This is not an easy change for an organization to go through, but it is essential that its structure stay up-to-date with the demands placed on it by a changing marketplace.

Too much management is also seen as a common problem. The current opinion is that three to five layers is the maximum number any organization should have. If you have more than that, the complexity of interdepartmental communication increases. There are more people to go through and to include, more people who can say no to a negotiated and peaceful settlement. Too many management layers also has a negative impact on innovation by slowing down the process and giving more people more turf to protect.

Often new layers are created in organizations to provide career paths and promotions for valuable employees. One area where there is definitely a need for more innovative thinking in organizations is finding *other* ways of rewarding valuable employees besides promotions. It is absurd to create a hierarchy that damages the organization just because it is the only way anyone can think of for rewarding achievement. When people are promoted, they are usually given an increase in salary. In most organizations, the only way to get the raise is to get promoted. Why not give these employees the money and leave the organization's structures alone! Then find other ways to give them public, status-oriented recognition in the company. I have watched many companies add one layer after another to the hierarchy simply to reward their talented employees. If you are fortunate enough to have the problem of too many talented employees to reward, make sure you reward them well—but do not do it by creating an unnecessary maze of management and tribes.

PHONE SYSTEMS

Phone systems can fan the flames of interdepartmental conflict, or they can help to ease it. Features such as conference-calling and good transferring systems can be used to link tribes—or they can be used to get rid of people. A common practice in businesses is what I have heard called "here you go!" transferring. People do not stay on the line to explain the transfer, they just shoot the caller off into oblivion. This creates more transfers, wasted time, and all-around irritation. Again, the stage is set for tribal warfare.

The internal telephone directory may encourage or discourage cross-tribal contact. In one company, most people know each other by first names only and are often confused by the complicated range of technical departments listed. A new directory was published recently with an alphabetized listing of all employees by *last* name. Departments were also listed by their official names, with no explanation of functions or information on who to call for what. People are hoarding their old directories and making pencil corrections as jobs turn over. Or employees simply ignore the directory completely and call only two or three people they trust for everything, whether the calls relate to their jobs or not.

BUDGETS

Another structural issue that can have an impact on the level of turf protection and can encourage or discourage tribal warfare is the budgeting process used by your organization. Each tribe has its own budget that it must defend from outside "robbery." When a project is developed that requires the participation of two or more tribes, there is trouble. Whose budget pays for the project? The organization has no pools of money or resources for joint efforts. If you tell people to cooperate, negotiate, and work together smoothly, and then set up your budgets to reinforce the strict turf boundaries, you have given a mixed message. In my experience, people will usually pay much more attention to the budget message than to the cooperation message. Innovation between the tribes will be the biggest casualty if your budgeting system is too tribal and rigid. As discussed earlier, new ideas almost always cross traditional turf lines. If those new ideas threaten to usurp tribal dollars, warfare is a high probability.

There are many ways to address the issue of budget protection or competition. The most common approach is to use top-management budgets to fund cross-departmental projects. Another approach is to set up an innovation budget or pool that can be used to fund new ideas. A department or person often manages the allocation of this money, based on the merit of the ideas. You can also use a reward system in which a tribe gets some kind of resource credit (money, people, space) for successful cross-tribal efforts. The tribe contributes part of its budget now, but gets a payoff later if the effort is a success for the company.

There are many other strategies for handling cross-tribal funding, but the point is that something needs to be done to ensure that the budget issue does not trigger conflict. People in tribes do not give up part of their budget out of the goodness of their hearts. Contrary to popular opinion, people in organizations *do* usually treat their portion of the company's money as if it was their own. They are emotional about it, and very protective.

PERFORMANCE APPRAISAL SYSTEMS

Performance appraisal systems rarely put much emphasis on an employee's interdepartmental negotiation skills. There are often a few references to teamwork and cooperation in a typical appraisal, but they are vague and relatively meaningless. Even if teamwork goals are taken seriously in the performance appraisal system, these goals usually are for good teamwork within tribes, not between tribes.

Even when negotiation skills are covered by the performance appraisal system, these skills then need to be tied to meaningful rewards. If you have a performance appraisal system that is vague, inspires only "going through the motions," and has very few meaningful rewards attached to it, then you are similar to the majority of organizations. You are not getting much mileage out of your system on *any* issue, including that of interdepartmental teamwork. If this is the case, I would first ask you: Are your managers and supervisors held accountable for—and appraised on—how well they carry out performance appraisals of their subordinates? This is usually not a key element of a supervisor's own performance appraisal. Performance appraisal is often ignored and treated as a dreaded task to be delayed as long as possible and then raced through as quickly as possible when it cannot be avoided any longer. This attitude sends the message to everyone in the organization that performance appraisals are unimportant. A powerful tool for building high-quality, well-functioning teams is thrown away when this happens.

EMPLOYEE AND DEPARTMENTAL SURVEYS

Most companies have some kind of employee attitude surveys or internal departmental assessments in which everyone rates other areas as well as their own area. If you use these surveys take a look at the questions on them and think about the issue of war or peace between the tribes. Ideally, the questions should ask for positive examples of cooperation and successful negotiation. A high percentage of the questions should clearly communicate the message that tribal warfare is not the way to do business in this organization. Most surveys that I have seen are either neutral on this issue or actually foster competition and bitter feelings between groups. "I'll get them on the next survey" is a far more common statement than "I'll remember that favor they did for me so I can put it on the next survey."

A second aspect of these surveys to think about is how the data are gathered and fed back to the employees. If the survey is done as a paper-and-pencil questionnaire once every year or so, most of the comments you receive will be about events that occurred in the preceding two or three weeks. It usually requires some discussion and tribal group meetings to gather accurate answers that can be used as constructive, helpful feedback to other tribes about their behavior. The paper-and-pencil approach will give you a fairly accurate snapshot of the *current* attitudes and conflicts, but it will rarely uncover the issues brewing under the surface, give you an accurate historical picture of what's happened during the survey period, or reveal *any* positive information.

Surveys are usually used as complaint sheets. After they are tabulated, examine how the data are returned to the people who filled them out. Secret surveys—in which employees are asked to give information but never hear about any of the results—foster paranoia and stress. If feedback is given to the employees and tribes, however, it is very important that it be done so as to reward successes and suggest solutions for problem areas. The survey data should only be used as a catalyst for discussion and problem-solving between tribes, not as a new weapon. Have a good referee who can keep the meetings on a constructive path.

If you are trying to conserve cost, skip the paper, the pencils, the computer, and the company-wide effort. Face-to-face contact will give you your return on investment in this area. If you can afford the full-blown survey process and companywide effort, then all the better. Just be careful how you use it. The most common mistake made by organizations is in thinking that a survey can substitute for human contact. It cannot, and it never will.

PARTIES AND CONFERENCES

Most organizations have parties, picnics, birthday celebrations, or holiday celebrations. To determine if you are getting any tribal benefits from these events, ask yourself one question: Are the parties and events any fun? If company parties and events are not really fun—more a company obligation—then the cross-tribal benefits will probably be minimal. People will continue to show up for the required minimum time, talk to a few people they are already comfortable with, and then leave.

Making these events enjoyable and organizing activities that will get the various tribes mixing, playing, and laughing will be well worth the effort. Be careful about making every company event revolve around sports. Hard as this may be for some of you to believe, there are many employees in every company who do not like to participate in sporting events! Vary the activities enough to cover a wide range of leisure interests. One celebration event that many sales-based organizations use to reward the top salespeople is a trip for the "winners." This is a good motivational technique within the sales tribe. It does, however, create greater distance between the sales tribe and every other tribe. There are some companies that take everyone on some of these trips. This is, of course, a very expensive way to encourage teamwork, but simpler versions of this idea may have some possibilities for bringing your tribes together.

Annual meetings or company conferences offer opportunities to bring tribes together in a way that builds relationships and educates each group about the functions and concerns of the others. This works particularly well when a company is small. Everyone is invited to attend, and the atmosphere is informal. Later, when the organization grows in size, it becomes too cumbersome to involve everyone. To solve this problem, the common decision is to cut back on who is invited. Only people above a certain level, only field personnel, or no more spouses are typical restrictions—all of which carry the message that only the "important" people are invited. These people usually represent only a few tribes from the organization. In fact, that is how the decision is made about who to invite and who to leave out—certain tribes are invited, and others are not.

From a tribal point of view, this is the worst strategy you could use to handle the problem of too many people attending the annual meeting or conference. The message sent out to many of the tribes and to most front-line employees is insulting. A golden opportunity for building rapport between tribes is lost. And possibly most important of all, the absentees are not participating in the discussion, speeches, and activities that focus on the umbrella values of the organization and its current priorities. These values and priorities are the most important tool you have to unite the tribes under a common cause and direction, but not everyone is there to hear it. NIH (Not Invented Here) is a likely outcome. Commitment comes from involvement, and not being important enough to invite to the company's big events almost certainly increases alienation, not commitment.

If you have grown into a company with thousands of employees, you probably still have the problem of too many people. My first suggestion is to ask yourself if that is really true. Are you certain that the organization is too big to gather in one place once a year? If you decide that it is too big, or that you cannot shut down your entire operation for several days, then use a strategy that does not damage the teamwork and commitment level of your employees. Move to regional meetings, or to several meetings a year with a mixture of tribes at each one. The ideal would be for everyone in the company to attend at least one values-oriented conference a year. If that presents a budget or time problem, then you can simply have each person attend fewer meetings. Just remember to keep *every*one involved.

NEWS AND GOSSIP

News travels well in every organization, in one way or another. It can have a positive, linking effect as it travels, or it can be destructive and divisive. Some avenues can be provided to manage the flow, at least to some extent. Newsletters, bulletin boards, and other such devices used for disseminating personal information as well as company news can be a positive source of information. "Hero" stories can be publicized, and the definition of a hero can be managed. Some companies that emphasize customer service have "spies" who witness customer encounters and then write stories for the company newsletter, describing employees' star moments. The employees will often claim to be embarrassed at seeing their names in print, but it is usually obvious that they are loving every minute of it.

Any official effort to spread news needs to be carefully managed to cross tribal lines. A newsletter that only praises one or two tribes widens the gap instead of closing it. Including as many groups as possible in the news is the key to using this structure to cross-tribal advantage.

QUESTIONS TO ASK ABOUT YOUR
ORGANIZATION'S STRUCTURE

Does your organization have its own version of the "upstairs-down-stairs syndrome"? Are all the tribes clustered on separate floors? Is there a feeling that "we never see any of those people on the other floors or in the other buildings"? If each person feels "at home" in only one building or on one floor, then you are probably suffering from the upstairs-downstairs syndrome. Think about ways to create more of a melting-pot environment—rearranging the offices, moving senior management, or mixing the tribes. If your tribes maintain a very strong sense of "my turf/your turf," then the likelihood of conflict will be increased.

How far can you see from any one spot in the building? Do you see closed doors while looking up and down an empty corridor, or can you see in all directions—into offices, meeting rooms, and stairways? Go and stand in several different places in your building and count how many people you can see at each of them. Then count how many tribes those people represent. You may be able to see several employees, but are they all from one tribe? In many buildings you can go all day and never see anyone from another tribe.

What are the watering holes in your building? Are there places for breaks, meals, or brief conversations? Obviously, a balance needs to be reached between socializing time and productive time. But often loitering has been so discouraged that there are no comfortable or enjoyable places to chat or to see other people. Usually this does not stop the socializing, which just moves into the offices and cubicles. This is probably the last place you want socializing to occur in.

After you have identified your watering holes, check to see which tribes use each one. Even the lunchroom is not likely to be used consistently by representatives of all tribes. Each spot usually draws certain tribes and not others. Also check to see if the tribes ever mingle at these watering holes. Do you ever see representatives from more than one tribe at a table together in the lunchroom or break room?

Does everyone stand and stare straight ahead while riding elevators in your building, or do they talk and joke? Who talks with whom? When certain people get on does all conversation stop or move to the weather?

If you have features such as conference-calling and good transferring in your phone system, are they used to link tribes? Do people use the "here you go!" method for transferring calls, leaving the caller confused and irritated after repeating his request umpteen times?

Are your parking lots stratified so that the tribes with the most status get the best spots? Premium parking spots are used in some organizations as rewards for employees the best customer or tribal skills.

Does your budgeting system contribute to turf protection and tribal warfare? Whose budget pays for a project that requires the participation of two or more tribes? Does your organization have any pools of money or other resources to apply to joint efforts? If you tell people that joint efforts between tribes are important, but create a budgeting system that fosters turf protection, the tribes will believe the budget message.

Does your performance appraisal system evaluate teamwork and cross-tribal cooperation in a meaningful way? Is your appraisal terminology specific and understandable to the tribes? What are your rewards for successful cooperation and teamwork? An even more basic question, of course, is whether your organization has a performance appraisal system that works at all well on any issue. If, in your opinion, your performance appraisal system is generally inadequate, ask yourself if the managers and supervisors are evaluated on how well they carry out appraisals of their subordinates. Are they evaluated on both the quality and the timeliness of their appraisals? If they are not, then the message is that regular, high-quality performance appraisals are not really very important.

If you have an employee attitude survey or internal assessment, do its questions ask about interdepartmental communication? Does it ask for positive examples of cooperation or successful negotiations between groups? What percentage of the questions communicate the message that tribal warfare is not the way to do business in your organization? Do you have any way of getting information from this survey about events over the whole past year? Or do people tend to comment only on the recent events that they can easily remember? Do you have a feedback and problem-solving process in place so that the tribes can get together, review their feedback with each other, and look for joint solutions? Surveys can be an excellent tool for resolving tribal conflicts, or they can be used as just one more weapon to be used by the tribes against each other.

Are your parties, celebrations, and conferences effective in bringing your tribes together? Are they fun? Do people look forward to them or are they an obligation and a nuisance? Do your conferences and annual meetings include all your tribes, or only a few high-status groups in your organization? If including more people presents a budget problem, then ask yourself what kind of event you could have that would use the same budget but include everyone. There may be more possibilities than you realize.

How does news travel in your organization? Do you have any devices, such as newsletters or bulletin boards, that can be used for non-official information or is the rumor mill the only source for this news? If you have a newsletter, take a few back issues and count how many tribes are talked about in these issues. Do you have a broad cross-section of tribes represented, or only a few that are mentiond over and over?

How many layers of management do you have in your organization, and how many tribes? There is no "best" number, so the question of whether you have too many has to be answered differently for each organization. When you have a valuable employee who you want to retain and reward, is promotion the only real reward that you have to offer? Is it the only way to give that employee a substantial pay increase? Are new layers of management ever created as a reward. Are all your management layers structural necessities that benefit the company? How does your company reward valuable employees (including money) without creating unnecessary management layers?

The questions asked in this chapter get at only a few of the ways that the structures of an organization can hurt or help in the effort to bring the tribes together. Each organization has its own traditions, policies, and structures that need to be considered. The question to keep asking is, "Does this way of doing things bring the tribes closer together, or drive them further apart?" The goal is to bring the tribes into contact with each other in pleasant, productive, and interesting ways. It is much harder to do deadly battle with someone today if you laughed with him yesterday.

13 TRIBAL ETHICS

Ethics are closely tied to the values and rules of the game by which tribes operate. An organization may have unethical basic values in the sense that it produces poor-quality products or services, or treats its customers and vendors unfairly or dishonestly. But the subject of ethics comes up more often in discussions of *how* an organization carries out its values—what choices are made when hard decisions are called for.

Some tribes have developed destructive values or rules. Producing shoddy products, lying to customers, double-crossing your peers, or scapegoating your subordinates, all these represent values and rules that most of us would agree are harmful to the organization and are clearly unethical. Other values and rules fall into the "gray areas" where tribes may not agree on the most acceptable and ethical approaches. Gray areas require negotiating between the tribes.

In a health care setting, for instance clinical concerns will often lead some toward advocating higher staffing levels, longer stays in the hospital for patients, and many extra precautionary tests. Those with financial concerns will focus on streamlined, efficient operations and on keeping all costs under control, including staffing and treatment procedures. It takes a blending of the two perspectives to produce a hospital or clinic that not only provides high-quality clinical care but will stay in business from one year to the next. But if these two sets of tribes do not know how to migrate, the ethical considerations will rarely be addressed effectively.

Tribal warfare is not a good setting for sorting out ethical codes of behavior and policies for the organization. Sometimes any decision that is made has advantages and disadvantages—or is partially right and partially wrong. Deciding what standards to use and how to apply them as fairly as possible in a specific situation can be a very difficult task. Unless the organization itself sets clear and positive ethical standards, tribal standards are free to develop along neutral or negative paths. In the absence of such organizational standards, there will also be fewer ethical beliefs held in common by the tribes, so that tribal warfare is more likely to occur.

Much of the current research indicates that people think that business and industry are not doing a very good job of promoting ethical behavior. Whether or not these opinions are accurate is difficult to say, but there is no doubt that the perception is a bleak one. One of the questions asked in this research is whether or not businesses are pressuring their employees to engage in unethical behaviors to get the job done. And if this does occur, is it more of a problem than in the past? According to many of the opinion surveys done recently, the public's answer to both of these questions seems to be yes.

ETHICAL BANKRUPTCY?

In a recent *Wall Street Journal* survey, senior executives were asked whether people are unethical in their business dealings. Only 16 percent answered that unethical behavior seldom occurs. The other 84 percent said that people are unethical more often than not (3 percent), often (15 percent), or occasionally (66 percent).[1] In another survey conducted by sociologist Robert Allen, participants were asked their opinion about the statement, "Organizations in our society tend to encourage their members to behave unethically, dishonestly, and inhumanely in relationship to one another." Sixty-five percent of the respondents agreed with this statement. Another 20 percent believed that organizations were ethically neutral, when "neutrality" was defined as supporting either positive or negative ethical behavior as long as the organization's best interest came first. Overall, less than 10 percent of the 1,500 people surveyed thought that organizations encouraged their members to behave ethically.[2]

In this same study, people were also asked to review a list of organizations and institutions and to indicate which, if any, they believed were likely to encourage the practice of poor ethics by their

Table 13–1.   Percentage of Those Agreeing That Certain Institutions
Encourage Poor Ethics.

Institutions	Percentage
Business	79
Government agencies	76
Political parties	74
High schools	65
Colleges and universities	62
Athletic teams	58
Professional associations	52
Elementary schools	49
Communities	43
Hospitals	41
Churches	36
Families	30

Source: Reprinted, by permission of the publisher, from Robert F. Allen, "The IK in the
Office," *Organizational Dynamics* (Winter 1980): 30, © 1980 American Management Association, NY. All rights reserved.

members. Families were given the best rating of all organizations or
groups, although fully 30 percent of the respondents believed that
families encourage poor ethics. Business, government, and politics
received the worst scores, with approximately 75 percent of the respondents believing that these institutions encourage poor ethics.

In a study at the University of Pennsylvania, 2,000 people in ten
countries were given a hypothetical case study about a drug company.
They were asked to predict whether or not the company's executives
would decide to remove a drug from the market after they received
confidential information that the medication could be dangerous or
even lethal. All respondents believed that the company would continue
to market the drug, although 97 percent believed that this decision
would be unethical. The study concluded that the people surveyed
believe that most managers see the profits of their company as a higher
priority than its ethics.[3]

DO WE KNOW RIGHT FROM WRONG?

According to Irving Kristol, the well-known social critic and a professor
at New York University's Graduate School of Management, there is no
indication that business executives have any difficulty understanding

right from wrong.[4] They know the difference and consistently develop corporate codes for acceptable behavior that reflect their understanding. These ethical codes are very similar from one corporation to another, and they reflect some of the most basic forms of "right" behavior in our society. These codes often deal with issues such as honesty and fairness in business practices. In a sales organization, you do not sell products to the customer that he does not need, and you do not prospect in a fellow salesperson's territory. It would be a rare salesperson who does not understand these codes. Assuming that they know the codes and understand them, the real question is, do they do what is right according to these codes? Kristol asserts that getting people to do what is right and to not do what is wrong is the heart of the problem.

He goes on to describe a disturbing trend in the teaching of ethics, particularly at the university and graduate school level. The philosophy of "ethics" os no longer commonly equated with the teaching of "morals." It is now approached as a "values-free" subject concerned only with the use of logical, objective thinking to explore behavior choices. The "value systems" of various cultures and communities are examined, but without being "judgmental." Kristol claims that this focus probably does very little damage at the college level because most value systems are already formed by that age.[5]

Although I share some of Kristol's concerns, I do not necessarily agree that this approach to teaching ethics is useless or harmful. The problem is that it does not take the student far enough in the process of ethical thinking. The use of objective logic and cultural comparisons is an excellent way for students to broaden their thinking and to become aware that there may be many more ways to reach the right solution than they had previously realized. Technical or professional training often has a narrowing effect on an individual's thinking; it can teach you to think like a good tribal member, that is, within the acceptable tribal boundaries. Without some specific ethical training to broaden their horizons, many well-trained tribal members will end up being quite convinced that they have the *one* right answer to most business decisions. If you doubt this, sit through a meeting in almost any company with the chief financial officer, the director of marketing, and the head of internal operations. Unless these three people have been trained to view their company and business in general from a perspective broader than that of their own tribes, there will be many collisions between them about the right business methods and outcomes.

But, if you go no further in your ethics training effort than broadening your students' perspectives, you have not finished the job. You would leave people at a point where they could easily justify almost any behavior that would accomplish their goals. You cannot avoid the difficult task of sorting through the broad range of ideas and strategies available to you and determining which ones are acceptable ethical behavior in the business setting.

CHANGES IN THE WAY WE DO BUSINESS

Is business behavior worse than it used to be? The widespread answer to that question is yes. Many people seem to believe that our ethical standards are lower today than in the past. But others will contradict this common opinion and claim that it is simply nostalgic. These people are firmly convinced that human nature is the same as it has always been, and that the mix of honest and dishonest behavior is about the same as it was in the past. There are some changes that are occurring in American culture, however, that are worth considering. Although these changes certainly do not alter basic human nature, they do create a climate in which unethical or dishonest choices are easier to make.

Changes in American society that have had an effect on our ethical behavior are described by sociologist Robert Bellah in his book, *Habits of the Heart*.[6] He believes that these changes have made it increasingly difficult for us to understand and carry out the commitments in our lives. Over the past 100 years or so, we have moved from being a culture of small businesses, small towns, and farms to being a culture of large corporations, bureaucracies, and cities. One effect of this change is the division of an individual's life into separate and distinct spheres: home and work. In the farm or small-business setting of the past, home and work often blended together in a way that made it hard to tell where one left off and the other began. There are, of course, some people who still work at home, but the vast majority of America's work force is now made up primarily of managers and employees accountable for corporate profits and subject to bureaucratic policies, rather than independent business people accountable to their family, church, and local community.

The distinction between our corporate lives and our personal lives is clear-cut. Ethics (or morals) tend to fit more easily into the home/personal sector than into the work/business sector. If you recall one of the earlier survey statistics, 79 percent of the respondents felt that business encourages poor ethics, while only 30 percent believed that families suffer from this problem. There is a 50 percent gap between those two figures! And yet for the most part, the *same people* are living in both settings. The only difference is that one is lived in between 8 a.m. and 5 p.m. on workdays, and the other in the evenings and on weekends. This brings us back to Kristol's point that we know the difference between right and wrong, we just are not acting on that knowledge—especially in the work place.

THE ETHICAL GRAY AREAS

The choices that we have to make are often not so clear-cut that the simple question "Do we know right from wrong?" will be adequate to solve the dilemma. Sir Adrian Cadbury, chairman of Cadbury Candy Company, describes an ethical decision made by his grandfather when he was running the company. The decision was relatively clear ethically. Queen Victoria placed an order of a special run of chocolates in special decorative tins, to be sent to the soldiers serving in South Africa at the time. Cadbury was deeply opposed to the Boer War, and to fill the order was a violation of his personal beliefs. On the other hand, the additional work for his factories would be a great benefit for his employees. He resolved the issue by accepting the order, but filling it at cost. In this way, he provided his employees with the extra work, but did not profit from a war that he considered unjust. [7] His grandson asks, however, what would have happened if this company had been publicly held, with stockholders to consider. Many of those stockholders would have supported the war and certainly would have wanted to see the company make a profit from the work. The decision would not have been so clear-cut.

   When decisions are not easily resolved from an ethical point of view, there are many different ways to think through the dilemma. Cadbury suggests a two-step approach that helps you to clarify where you stand on the ethical issue involved. The first step is to ask yourself what your personal rules of conduct are. He stresses that this does not mean coming up with a vague set of flowery statements that sound like a "watered-down version of the Scriptures without their literary merit." Instead look back on actual decisions that you have made in the past and determine what your rules were that supported those decisions.

These rules should be an accurate barometer of your past behavior, not a list of high-flown principles that have nothing to do with what you might actually do in the future. The second step is to think about who else may be affected by your decision and how their interests should be weighted.[8] In other words think about the other tribes' points of view, whether they be internal, such as other departments, or external, such as customers or society at large. These two sets of answers can then be used as the basis for a decision that will achieve the best balance possible.

THREE ETHICAL NORMS FOR DECISION MAKING

Another way of making difficult ethical decisions is to use the standard approaches that have been developed by professional ethicists.[9] Each approach uses different criteria to evaluate the ethics of a particular behavior or situation.

Utilitarian Approach

Taking the utilitarian approach, you base decisions on the effects that they would have on the welfare of everyone. In other words, actions are judged by their consequences. An act is moral if it produces the greatest good for the greatest number of people. A manager using the utilitarian approach to make an ethical decision must ask, which alternative will produce the most good for the largest number of people? The decision that may produce the highest profits or the greatest market share may not be good for the customers or for the public. For example, layoffs and swift elimination of departments might be a likely outcome of taking the utilitarian approach to a situation that called for staffing reductions. The ethical decision, from this perspective, would be the one that produced the greatest benefit to stockholders, customers, and possibly even the remaining employees.

Individual Approach

This kind of approach emphasizes the importance of individual rights. It is assumed that human beings have certain moral rights that should be respected in all decisions. This approach to ethical thinking is familiar to every American who has read the Bill of Rights and subsequent amendments to the Constitution. These basic rights include privacy, free speech, due process under law, freedom of religion, habeas corpus, a free press, and so on.

The rights approach to making ethical decisions is easier than the utilitarian approach because the criteria are more clear-cut. If the decision violates any individual's rights, then it is unethical. A manager using the rights approach would consider each person affected by the decision. This approach protects the individual from exploitation and establishes standards for behavior that are based on valued societal principles, but it can be problematic where efficiency and productivity are concerned.

Using the same example of a company faced with the need for staff reductions, the rights approach would focus much more on the individual employees who are likely to be affected by layoffs. A decision might be made to downsize gradually through attrition and job relocation, even if this meant carrying extra expense for an extended period of time, resulting in smaller pay increases for employees and diminished returns for investors.

Distributive Justice

This approach focuses on fairness and emphasizes equal treatment of individuals who are similar to one another in job-related qualities. The benefits and burdens of ethical decisions are equally distributed. Many of the fair labor laws are based on this approach and require that an employer treat all employees equally in hiring, promoting, firing, pay, and so on.

The justice approach can be difficult to apply because it is often difficult to determine whether two different situations are equal. When the circumstances are not identical, the fair thing to do is not always obvious. Determining what would be "equal treatment" in discipline situations, for instance, is often difficult. No two situations are ever the same. You must look at the basic rules and determine whether they were clearly spelled out and communicated.

If you attempt to apply the distributive justice approach to the staff reductions situation, the primary concern would become equal treatment of all employees. Layoffs might occur, but the emphasis would be on fair treatment and on even-handedly using seniority as a basis for the decision about who would be terminated. Severance pay and out-placement services would be offered on an equal basis to all employees of the same rank.

These three approaches to making difficult ethical decisions cannot be used as anything more than blueprints. At different times a person could go in any one of the three directions. At other times, there would be conflict between the three approaches. A decision may protect an individual's rights, but not provide the best good for the most people. The manager is forced to choose between the two outcomes.

The value of this kind of blueprint, however, is that it gives you a way to think about your own personal priorities. Most people have a clear preference for one of these three approaches and can probably rank them from their most preferred approach to their least preferred. This helps to answer that question that Cadbury encourages people in business to ask themselves: What are your own personal rules of conduct? Are you more likely to opt for a decision that (1) provides the greatest good for the greatest number of people, (2) protects individual rights, or (3) is just and fair, in that it treats everyone equally?

ASSESSING YOUR ORGANIZATIONAL AND TRIBAL VALUES AND RULES

Without a clear understanding of what the values are in your organization, it will be difficult, if not impossible, to guide the ethical behavior of your employees and tribes. Chapter 4 took you through a series of steps that help to identify tribal and organizational umbrella values. That is the first step toward managing ethical behavior.

You can examine your lists of umbrella and tribal values to see if they directly address ethical issues, such as honesty and humane treatment of employees, customers, vendors, and others. The definition of quality that is probably a part of your organization's values needs to clearly state what "doing right" means in your company. Many companies are ethically neutral in their behaviors. The message is that either ethical or unethical behavior is acceptable, so long as good results are produced for the company. If there is a history of ethical and unethical behavior being equally tolerated and even rewarded in your organization, then neutrality is probably the message that employees are hearing.

Rewarding Ethical Behavior

A list of values is only meaningful if people believe that the organization is serious about them. The best indicator to employees and tribes of what is really important is seeing who gets rewarded and for what. In one major corporation that has thousands of employees and hundreds of tribes, the printed corporate statement of mission and values is an eloquent and impressive philosophical statement of ethical behavior. There are a number of tribes—mostly remote-site field operations—that consistently try to carry out these values in their day-to-day work. The corporate headquarters, on the other hand, has a history of rewarding some of its most ruthless and politically savvy employees. Although there are some top managers who are models of ethical behavior, there are at least as many who are known for their tyrannical treatment of employees and for their political plotting to enhance their own power.

If you asked all the employees in that company headquarters the question, "Does your organization encourage its members to behave ethically, honestly, and humanely in their relationships with one another?" I am quite certain that most would answe be "No," or "Neutral." This company is neutral; it supports either positive or negative ethical behavior, as long as outcomes are in the organization's best interest.

I think this assessment would not be unusual for many, if not most, organizations. If you surveyed most corporate employees about their own companies, asking that same question, "neutral" is likely to be the highest percentage response. There is in fact a common corporate expression which is not printable, describing what "floats to the top." Anyone who has worked in corporate settings has heard it and understands the metaphor. The expression does not always describe accurately who makes it up the corporate ladders, but it does accurately express organizationwide cynicism about ethics and their importance to the success of the company.

If you want ethical behavior, consistently reward the people who use it and model it for the company. Find the people who excel in their fields *and* are ethical in their methods. Then praise them, promote them, and pay them well.

Notice that I have not mentioned punishing or sanctioning unethical or dishonest behavior. This is, of course, an important way to reinforce ethical behavior and to protect the organization. The reason that I do not stress sanctions is that, as a strategy to promote ethical behavior, they are not at all as powerful as rewards. Positive reinforcement—rewards and praise—draw people like a magnet to the individuals, behaviors, or events that triggered it. Negative reinforcements—sanctions and firing—may teach everyone a lesson, but leave them fearful about whether they will be next. This is especially true if you sanction a behavior that the informal rules have led people to believe is a legitimate strategy for getting the job done. The head of a large public utility company fired a manager because he had been caught "fudging" production statistics.[10] The head later found out that the other managers on the same level as the man who had been fired were very upset. It was then discovered that the manager had been fired for a behavior that was considered normal and acceptable under the rules of the production manager tribe. In fact, if he had not fudged figures, he probably would have been fired sooner because all the others were lying about their figures and his would have been unacceptably low.

Migrating as Ethical Behavior

For the most part, the skills of migrating and linking individuals and tribes are dealt with in this book as practical issues. These skills produce the results you want, as quickly as possible, and with as little hassle as possible. Organizational tribes that know how to migrate and are willing to use these skills have less tribal warfare, less stress, and higher levels of productivity. Migrating and linking are simply good business strategies.

But there is another side to the skill of migrating that is equally important. The ability and willingness to migrate, to look at issues through the other person's eyes, and to find ways to link two opposing sides is a behavior that in itself is "doing right." Migrating promotes ethical behavior. If two people from different tribes are negotiating about how to resolve a customer problem, there is a much higher probability that the problem will be fixed accurately and quickly if the two sides make a genuine effort to migrate and to understand each other's point of view. The two tribes would thus be allies working to address a customer concern, rather than adversaries pitted against each other in a win-lose situation. The underlying values of this behavior—fair play, empathy, tolerance—are some of our most basic societal values. Most six-year-olds can already tell you that you should treat people the way you want to be treated. The smartest pragmatic strategy is also ethical, honest, and humane.

QUESTIONS TO ASK ABOUT TRIBAL ETHICS

Do you see your organization and your tribe as being ethical, unethi-cal, or ethically neutral? Can you point to examples of all three kinds of decisions—utilitarian, individual, and distributive justice—that have been made in your organization, or is there a predominance of one or the other of them? What do people get rewarded for in your organization? Do rewards it have anything to do with ethics, or is that not a significant issue when it comes to rewards? If a company wants to stress the importance of ethical behavior, it needs to be talked about, written about, modeled, and rewarded. Otherwise, ethics are at best, a back-ground issue and may not be taken very seriously by most employees and tribes within the organization.

Using Cadbury's two-step process for clarifying your own ethical standards, ask yourself the following questions:

1. *What are your personal rules of conduct?* Base your answer on examples of your actual behavior in the past. Think of several tough ethical decisions that you had to make and decide what you think were the underlying principles that guided your decisions.
2. *What groups and individuals will be affected by a decision you are currently facing?* You will have to decide how to weight the different interests of the various people affected. Once you have de-termined your own rules of conduct and the various interests of the people affected by your decision, then you can use this information as the data with which to make the decision. The decision may still be a difficult one, but at least you have thought through the circum-stances in a rational way that may be helpful.

Of the three ethical approaches, which one do you to prefer? Every-one probably uses some aspect of all three, but you may be able to say which one is your preferred approach to ethics. Try to think of examples of how you might use each one in a business decision.

Do your umbrella values and tribal values communicate the message you want them to about ethical behavior?

Do your umbrella and tribal values directly address issues such as honesty and humane treatment of employees and others?

Do your definitions of quality make it clear what "doing right" means in you company?

Would a new employee be able to read your list of values and know that this is a company that is not "neutral" on ethics? If you find gaps in your values descriptions, revise them. Add the missing elements. If it is true that most people know what is right and wrong, spotting the gaps and figuring out how to fill them should not be difficult.

Is ethical behavior rewarded in your organization? Can you think of times when a person has received recognition specifically for his ethical behavior? Or times when a person's ethical behavior was at least a part of what earned him a reward? When you look at those in the senior ranks of your organization is it obvious that ethics is one of the requirements for "doing well" in your organization? An organization gets what it pays attention to and rewards. Rewarding is the most powerful tool available to produce the kind of behavior that is valued. It has a much more lasting effect than punishment ever will.

III OTHER BUSINESS TRIBES

14 INFORMAL ORGANIZATIONAL TRIBES

In the first two sections of this book, the focus has been on departmental or functional tribes in the organization. All of us, however, are members of many different tribes, both at work and in our personal lives. When you leave work at the end of the day, your language, values, thinking, and rules probably go through some significant changes as you return to your personal tribe.

In addition to personal tribes, there is almost always more than one tribe that we belong to at work. Many of these tribes are informal and do not show up on any organizational chart. An individual must balance loyalties to these various groups. This can become very difficult if the characteristics of these tribes are in conflict. For example, the quality control tribe may tell an employee to protect quality by setting aside any defective products for internal correction. But the values of his informal friendship tribe may tell this employee not to rat on his friends. This conflict in values forces the employee to choose between two different loyalties and will usually trigger a great deal of stress. As a manager it is important to be aware of the informal tribes so that you can anticipate the conflicts that may occur and structure procedures that reduce these forced-choice dilemmas as much as possible.

Several different kinds of tribes are described below. As you read about them, try to identify your own informal tribal memberships. Think of conflicts that could occur, when you would have to choose between your loyalties to two different groups. Then ask yourself how you might be able to reconcile the demands of the two tribes. In other words, it is possible to at least reduce the gap between two groups' positions, even if you cannot totally eliminate the conflict. Sometimes, however, you just have to choose one or the other and live with the consequences of that choice. Making those choices can be some of your most stressful decisions.

FRIENDSHIP TRIBES

Friendship tribes are among the most powerful tribes in any organization. Employee loyalties will often be clearly aligned with these tribes. When put in a forced-choice situation, many employees will consistently choose to honor their friendship tribe's rules or values.

Sometimes these tribes overlap with the departmental or functional tribes. Nurses are friends with nurses, flight attendants with flight attendants, bank tellers with bank tellers, and so on. Often, however, friendship tribes are smaller. For example, there may be several friendship tribes within the ranks of all accounting clerks in a large corporate department. Internal conflict within a department often has as much to do with battles between the friendship tribes as it does with "personality clashes." Friendships can also occur, of course, between people from different job functions, but these usually occur individually and are quite different from the tight groups of employees in the same line of work who stick together. Individual, cross-functional friendships rarely constitute a tribe.

Turnover of personnel or major restructuring may disrupt these informal tribes, but under normal circumstances they can go on for years. One of the key sources of resistance to change in organizations is fear of losing these friendship tribes. Something as simple as a change in scheduling of employee hours—with no change in function, number of hours, or routines—can have a very disruptive effect on these tribes. Employees will give you all sorts of elaborate objections to the schedule changes, but the issue may well be that you are disrupting their social relationships. This is not a superficial or unimportant concern. Much of the positive morale and motivation comes from the strength of personal relationships in the friendship tribes.

There are a number of strategies for handling necessary changes so as to reduce the resistance of informal tribes. As a rule of thumb, the best approach is usually to include as many people as possible in planning the change. In this way, they can see more clearly what is coming, can have some degree of control to protect their tribes, and can begin to form new relationships as they work on implementing the change. For example, a move from an old building is usually disruptive to the tribes. People are relocated, routines are different, and the watering holes change. Getting representatives of various tribes involved in the planning and execution of the move will produce better results than having everyone show up in the new building after the boxes are delivered to "discover" the new setting for the first time.

Sometimes the only available strategy for handling this resistance is to allow employees to vent their feelings about the changes. This strategy does not affect the circumstances, but at least it allows employee frustrations to be expressed so that they will dissipate as quickly as possible. This strategy is useful if there is no way to include people in the planning for the change. It may be a sudden, emergency change, or one that requires secrecy for some reason. If you need to implement these kinds of change, you are in much greater danger of tribal revolt, especially from the friendship tribes. If at all possible, take the time and effort to include some of these people in the planning before the change. That participation will go a long way toward protecting morale and productivity during and after the change.

GENDER TRIBES

Probably the most basic of all the tribes that we belong to are the male and female tribes. Men and women in our society have been raised in two separate subcultures. There have been many changes over the past few decades, and the differences between these two subcultures are a little more subtle now—but they still exist. Many people believe that some of the differences go beyond cultural training and are actually genetic. I will leave those theories and opinions for others to debate. The fact remains that men and women make up two distinct tribes, and this tribal membership affects their behavior within organizations. The general patterns of these two tribes are described below, using the five-part assessment tool described earlier. These descriptions are not intended, of course, to accurately describe any specific individual. The characteristics are a composite of general patterns for each group and are based on a vast number of research findings.

Tribal Characteristics

There are significantly more men who indicate left-brain thinking preferences and more women who indicate right-brain thinking preferences. There are also more men represented in the organizational tribes
that tend to use left-dominant thinking, such as medical, legal, engineering, and finance tribes. Likewise, there are more women represented in
the tribes that tend toward right-dominant thinking, such as personnel,
nursing, designer, and social worker tribes. There are, of course, many
exceptions to this general pattern, in both tribes and individuals. This
pattern is so pervasive, however, that my clients almost always point out
the gender significance of the left- and right-brain thinking patterns
before I even mention it.

1. Language and Dialect Differences.   The clearest way to see the
dialect differences between men and women in organizational settings
is to watch what happens when a one-gender group of people, who are
used to meeting together regularly, is suddenly joined by a new member
from the opposite sex. Many behavior changes occur, but language is
usually one of the most obvious adjustments.

I have experienced this language adjustment in my own corporate
experience. A number of years ago, I was asked to give a presentation
to a group of eight subsidiary presidents (all men) who met together
frequently and worked as a tight senior management team during these
meetings. I walked into the room where they were sitting at a round
table and pulled up a chair to join them. As soon as I sat down, I had the
overwhelming feeling that it had been a very long time since a woman
had been present at their meetings. There were many cues, but their
language patterns were what struck me first. They were polite, quieter
than I knew most of them to be, did not swear, and stopped most of their
typical verbal humor, their way of sparring with each other. As the
meeting progressed, they gradually reinstated some of these behaviors,
but there was still a feeling that "the brakes were on" throughout the
whole meeting.

Afterwards, I asked a male colleague who also attended the meeting
how long it had been since a woman had joined them. He was sure that
a few women had attended in the past, but he could not exactly
remember when. And yes, he agreed that their behavior and language
had been very different from what it was when males were invited to
give presentations.

It does not usually work well for either men or women to try to talk like the other gender. Speaking in a "foreign" tongue sounds strange and often ends up making everyone uncomfortable. It is usually simpler to try to use a modified version of both dialects. After a period of time, this mixed language can become as natural as any other tribal dialect. You hear this mixed language in evenly mixed groups of men and women who work together regularly. Language is usually not a problem because they have adopted a different dialect that minimizes the gender issue. Even in these groups, however, both men and women will often fall back into their gender specific dialect as soon as they are left alone together—even for short periods of time, such as in the bathroom or over lunch. One of the most thorough and effective training experiences in most people's lives was their early training in how to be a well-adjusted member of their gender subculture. We know appropriate gender behaviors so well that they happen on automatic pilot.

2. Tribal Values.   Even when men and women share the same basic values, they often organize their thinking about them differently. Ask a random sampling of men and women to describe themselves—to say who they are, or what their identity is. Figure 14–1 highlights some of the typical differences you will hear in their answers. There are, of course, many areas of overlap, but mainly there are a number of significant differences.

A man is more likely to say, "I want to get ahead in this company, and I don't care whether people like me or not" (achievement motivation). Women are more likely to say that they want success, but that they also

Figures 14–1.   Self-identification and Motivation, by Gender.

MEN	WOMEN
Identify themselves in terms of their occupation, status, and income	Identify themselves in terms of occupation, status, income, children, marriage, parents, friends, home
Primarily motivated by drive to achieve	Primarily motivated by a drive toward relationships and acceptance, or by a fusing of relationship and achievement motivations

Source: Harriet B. Braiker, *The Type E Woman: How to Overcome the Stress of Being Everything to Everybody* (New York: Dodd, Mead, 1986), p. 48.

want to be liked in general by others in the organization (achievement and relationship motivation). A worry that is expressed much more often by women than by men is whether "too much" emphasis on their own achievement needs will force them to forfeit social acceptance or satisfying relationships with men in their personal lives. Pick up any magazine for "working women" and you will notice the great number of articles about balancing achievement and relationship needs, both on and off the job. Then take a look at the magazines geared primarily to men. You will probably have to look through quite a few back issues before you will find similar articles. The magazines know their tribes, and their contents reflect the interests of their readers.

Just as with other organizational tribes, these values differences are a great source of conflict between men and women. Women often conclude that the men in their lives are "too narrow," too focused on achievement and their jobs. Men, on the other hand, insist that they do care about other values, but that they have to concentrate on their careers to be successful. "Something has to give" is a statement that I have heard over and over from men who I have known through my work. I rarely hear this statement from a woman. Considering the distance between these two positions, it is no surprise that negotiating over gender values differences can be an emotional and difficult task.

3. Training and Background Differences.   Although men and women often attend the same schools and mix in the same classes, male and female subcultures receive very different training and socialization. Almost any first- or second-grade child can tell you in detail the differences between feminine and masculine behavior. In addition to the behaviors that all of us can point to and describe easily, there are many, more subtle behaviors that operate subconsciously.

One such behavior that I have noticed in my communications work in organizations is what I call masculine and feminine "assertive" behavior. Using a positive example, let's assume that both a man and a woman are effectively and assertively using high-quality negotiation and communication skills. Even with their aggressive or passive tendencies under control, the style, word choices, and body language of men and women are distinctly different. (Let me be clear that I am *not* describing manipulative versions of assertive behavior, if there even is any such thing.)

I have also observed that if either gender digresses from these acceptable, gender-specific patterns for assertive behavior, there are a number of graphic and derogatory labels that are often used to describe that person's behavior. Any behavior that does not fit the expected pattern is irritating or offensive to many people, who usually respond by discounting what that person is saying and, if it happens frequently, discounting even the person. The punishment in our culture for straying from your gender tribe seems to be more severe than it is for any other tribal disloyalties, it can be meted out by one's own gender tribe as well as by the opposite tribe.

4. Thinking Pattern Differences.   As with all tribal differences, the first step in communicating and working together more smoothly can be to discover that there are four different ways of thinking, which all have something to offer—in other words, that there is no one "right" way to think, and three "wrong" ones. The second step is learning to migrate into all four kinds of thinking in response to different situations and people. Everyone uses all four kinds of thinking to some extent. Learning to use them more flexibly is not as painful as it may sound. You do not have to pack your bags and move into your nonpreferred quadrants—just "visit" a little more often! Migrating is an excellent way to break down some of the male-female tribal warfare that occurs in offices and homes.

5. Rules of the Game.   There are some significant differences between men and women in the rules of the game, according to the research done in this area. Figure 14–2 outlines a few of these differences, which are, in effect, different mottoes or rules for living, that men and women adopt. These also represent different approaches to work taken by men and women.

If men and women both claim that they are playing by the same rules when some of these fundamental "realities" are as different as those described in Figure 14–2, there is clearly the potential for serious misunderstanding.

Building bridges between the male and female tribes in our culture is important to the quality of life in businesses and organizations as well as in our families and friendships. Both tribes offer many valuable talents and skills that can be used to build more productive and innovative organizations. Learning how to use the visual, intuitive, interpersonal skills that traditionally women have excelled at is still new to many organizations. These skills can be powerfully combined with the resiliency, determination, and decisiveness that historically have

Figure 14–2. Rules of the Game, by Gender.

MALE	FEMALE
Driven by competition	Driven by perfectionism
Pressure to perform at all times	Pressure to please at all times
Attributes successes to own ability or hard work	Attributes successes to luck
Attributes failures to circumstances beyond control	Attributes failure to own lack of ability
Emphasis in marriage relationships on expectation of "primariness" (being the most important person to his mate)	Emphasis in marriage relationship on expectation of "permanence" (safe to have children with partner)
Guilt triggered by lack of success and job satisfaction	Guilt triggered by too much success and job satisfaction

Source: Harriet B. Braiker, *The Type E Woman: How to Overcome the Stress of Being Everything to Everybody* (New York: Dodd, Mead, 1986), p. 49; and Georgia Witkin-Lanoil, *The Female Stress Syndrome: How to Recognize and Live With It* (1984), p. 125 and *The Male Stress Syndrome: How to Recognize and Live With It* (1986), p. 146 (New York: Newmarket Press).

characterized male behavior. Focusing on both sets of "realities" in our organizations, and building on their strengths, is an important ingredient in producing the ideas, energy, and quality of work that every organization is searching for.

MISSION TRIBES

Sometime groups of people will band together for a period of time because of a common mission. This mission could be anything from implementing a new company service to serving as an employee grievance tribe. These tribes are usually temporary and disband when the mission is accomplished (or fails), but they exhibit many of the tribal characteristics described in this book during the time they are operating as a tribe.

Sometimes these mission tribes are sanctioned by management, such as those that are organized to develop new employee policies or to develop a new service or product for the company. Other times a mission tribe can spring up from the employee ranks, and management may actually be its adversary, as when employees feel that they have been treated unfairly in terms of pay, benefits, or working conditions. The important thing to realize about mission tribes is that they cannot be ignored. It is much safer to acknowledge their existence, communicate with them frequently, and keep them committed to the organization's larger mission as much as possible.

Because these groups are often temporary and very informal in their structure, they are easy to miss. If they are upset about an issue, they can have the entire organization or division in an uproar before anyone even notices that there is a "movement" in progress. The most effective way to deal with these groups is to communicate a great deal of information to them quickly and frequently. Even if the news that is communicated is not what they want to hear, keeping them informed and handling the situation in a fair, straightforward way will usually keep these tribes with a mission from starting a revolt.

I have heard over and over from employees in many organizations that "it is not *what* management did that upset us as much as *how* they did it." Usually they are referring to issues of communication and fairness. For example, if there is going to be a staff reduction that will affect everyone else's work load and schedule, it is important that as much information as possible be shared with employees as quickly as possible, whether it is good news or bad. People almost always handle bad news better than no news. When they get no news, they fill in the gaps themselves, using their imaginations to replace the missing facts. The imagined story is usually much worse than the truth could ever have been. This increases the risk that a mission tribe will be organized to resist the change, or at least to make the process more difficult than it might have been.

HOBBY TRIBES

These are usually more lighthearted tribes, that generate a lot of enthusiastic loyalty among their members and are often sports-related. Sports tribes are obvious during the World Series or during football season. Betting tribes are often a noisy and rowdy bunch. Golfing tribes are tight groups that have the power to include or exclude people from significant business contacts. Country clubs are the setting for distinct tribes and usually have a clear-cut pecking order in terms of status in the community.

These tribes generate many positive benefits for their participants. But they also have a negative side, usually for the people who are unable or not allowed to participate. If you are trying to build a network of tribes that work well together as a team, too much emphasis on the sports tribes, which include only certain people, can be destructive. It becomes a clear case of the inside-outside dynamic. Those on the inside are having a great time, but those on the outside not only feel left out but often end up feeling resentful or unvalued. The problem is that not everyone is interested or talented or wealthy enough to participate in many of these tribes. This does not mean, of course, that they should not exist. But as a manager, you should be careful about how much visibility and status are associated with these tribes. Having lots of different hobby tribes that many people can join is one way to address the potential problems.

COMMUNITY TRIBES

These tribes take on special importance in small towns and rural areas. I have worked in small-town organizations where it was very wise for me to spend some time learning who was related to whom among the employees. Relatives, long-running friendships, and scandals had serious effects on how people clustered into tribes and on how effectively they worked together. Church affiliations can be very important in some communities. These tribes are all in the background while employees are at work, but they have a powerful influence over attitudes about work and about each other.

The company rumor mill extends beyond the company walls in a small-town. False rumors, or the negative effects of any gossip, spread at even faster rates than in large, more anonymous settings. It is very important to "keep your mouth shut" if you want to stay out of the tribal cross fire. When there have been high levels of conflict in a department, the first thing that I suggest to its members is to stay off the internal telephone system and to quit talking about anything personal with anyone at work. Gossip can tear apart any group of people trying to work together as a team. It can be a nightmare of rumors, backbiting, and criticism.

On the other hand, organizations that have this kind of tight community feeling can be warm and friendly places to work. The question is whether or not employees use their knowledge of each other to be helpful and supportive, or to spread tribal warfare in the organization, as well as out into the community.

TRUST AND CORPORATE POLITICS

In the informal tribes the issue of trust is more apparent than it is with departmental, divisional, and functional tribes. Trust between tribes is important in all of these areas, but the importance of it is more obvious in the informal tribes. In many ways, the trust exhibited in informal tribes is a major benefit to the individuals, as well as to the organization. It is a basic form of support and acceptance that creates a positive working environment and fosters higher morale.

People can also use the informal tribes to accomplish what they want when the formal structures do not work or are not trustworthy. If talking directly to someone from another tribe does not end with a negotiated agreement, or if the formal hierarchy does not help to solve a problem, people will go to the informal network of relationships to try to have an impact. Because these tribes offer an alternative way of solving problems, they offer little discouragement to the "I don't trust them" theme you will often hear in conversations about other tribes. When I ask a group of managers a question about some intertribal problems they are having and get a room full of silent stares in response, it is fairly obvious that they do not trust each other. I can usually tell who it is they do not trust by roaming around at the break and seeing who is off in a corner with whom, discussing the issue in private. Those clusters are informal tribes that do trust each other. The people they are not talking to are the ones they do *not* trust.

Sometimes these informal tribes are successful at getting the problems solved on their own, but more often they offer only a safe place for letting off steam. To really address a problem, you have to get it out on the table and you have to deal with the other groups that are a part of it. In other words, informal tribes offer a good backup system for resolving conflicts and solving intertribal problems, but they do not work well if they are the primary route—or even worse, the only route—toward solving problems that anyone trusts. When this occurs, you have corporate politics at its worst. Informal tribes may provide good settings for individuals who want to build power bases for their own personal gain, but they do not promote companywide teamwork.

QUESTIONS TO ASK ABOUT INFORMAL TRIBES

In two or three large departments in your organization, who clusters with whom into friendship tribes in each department? People who are in friendship tribes eat lunch together, see each other outside of work, and know a great deal about each other's families and personal lives. Do these friendship tribes ever square off against each other? Are there any departmental policies that pressure employees into "betraying" the members of their friendship tribe? If you have policies that, directly or indirectly, force people to turn in their friends or get their friends in trouble in other ways, change the policies. Friendship tribes will always find ways to undermine these policies and will spend a great deal of time and energy doing it.

Do community tribes play a significant role in your organization? This is more likely to be an issue in small-town or rural settings, but it can occur anywhere. If people's affiliations with groups outside of work play an important role in who they trust at work, then community tribes are a significant force in your organization. Community tribes can be a positive force, fostering a warmer, more caring environment. Or they can be distractive, by intensifying gossip, scandal, and feuding. Which kind of influence do community tribes have in your organization? If they have a negative impact, slowing down the rumor mill is about the only strategy that will help. Moving employees to break up these groups during the workday can help as well. The negative impact of some community tribes, however, is a very difficult dynamic to change.

How many different hobby tribes do you have in your organization over the course of a year? Are they all sports-related, or is there a variety of tribes for people to join? These kinds of tribes can be fun and good for morale as long as they are not too exclusive. The significant question to ask is: How many people get to participate in these tribes?

Do you have any temporary mission tribes in your organization? The important thing to do with these tribes is simply to realize that they exist and that they have many of the same characteristics as other tribes. Do not ignore them. Communicating frequently and in depth with these tribes will help to keep them from going AWOL. The goal with mission tribes is to keep them tied to the organization and committed to the larger mission as much as they are to their own agenda.

Thinking of a number of men and women you know in your organization, can you identify differences between them in each of the five tribal characteristics?

- Language/Dialect
- Values
- Training and Background
- Thinking Patterns
- Rules of the Game

These differences can be either sources of conflict or ways to integrate a wider range of strengths to serve the organization. Recognizing gender differences and overcoming the assumption that the other tribe is always wrong are the first steps toward reducing conflict and building on strengths.

15 CUSTOMER TRIBES AND OTHER INDUSTRY TRIBES

Every organization has some kind of customer. A sales-based company has individual clients. A nonprofit association has its membership. Manufacturing companies have retailers or other manufacturers as customers. Most organizations have more than one customer group to deal with, and each group probably represents a different tribe, with its own language, values, rules, and other tribal characteristics.

Some other outside groups that play a significant role in your organization's day-to-day operations are the vendors and other industries that you have contact with in the process of doing business. They may be suppliers for your company, or providers of services that are essential to your ability to perform your function. These external tribes are not actually customers—they are not the market for your services or products—but they are groups that you have to negotiate with regularly. And they do not see the world in the same way that your internal tribes do. But the tribal perspective can be applied to these groups to improve your ability to communicate and negotiate effectively outside your organization as well as inside it.

CUSTOMER TRIBES

When a customer comes to your organization for service, that individual is representing various tribes. Tribal memberships are an important part of everyone's identity. The customer is much more likely to be comfortable around people who seem to understand his tribal connections.

There are categories of tribes that we all belong to and that are based on factors such as age, profession, religion, and socioeconomic status. At times, for instance, it can be helpful to relate to a customer as a young lawyer who lives in a certain section of the city. Assuming you know all about him, however, can get you into trouble. If you rely too much on stereotypes, you often stop listening to the real and unique person who is talking to you. Many people cannot be stereotyped—remember, that person belongs to many tribes and combines characteristics from all of them. Even if a customer epitomizes a certain tribe and all its characteristics, you will still have trouble on your hands if you stop listening. The customer will sense that you are not paying attention to him and will either end up feeling that he heard a canned speech or that you did not answer his specific questions and concerns. You have a dissatisfied customer in spite of your effort to notice his tribal connections and your attempt to respond to them in your conversation.

Responding to the Tribal Characteristics of Customers

Stereotyping a client is dangerous, but there are other ways to use tribal information to the customer's advantage as well as your own. Use the five tribal characteristics as guidelines for listening. If you are listening for the customer's dialect or thinking pattern, it will increase the intensity of your listening. You will be paying more attention to this particular person, and he will be aware of it.

Language and Dialect.   Listen for the client's jargon, or lack of it. If he does not understand your tribal lingo, you should translate your language for him, incorporating words he uses into your own speech. Imagine an insurance clerk talking to a customer about health insurance coverage. The clerk will use the terms *primary* and *secondary* insurance to refer to the two policies the customer carries. The customer, on the other hand, will probably call these policies "my company policy" and "my back-up coverage." I have seen many insurance clerks fail to pick up on this language gap. The clerk continues to use the terms *primary* and *secondary* throughout the conversation even though they are confusing to the customer. After all, the clerk's terms are more technically accurate. But one small opportunity to help close the customer-employee gap was lost.

Language differences between industries or companies can be a communication stumbling block. Your jargon and slang are meaningless outside your own industry. There are several strategies that can help reduce the static interference between internal and external tribes caused by language differences.

First, do not use your tribal dialect when talking to someone outside your industry. Where language is concerned, think of representatives of other industries in the same way you would think of customers. Dejargonize your speech. Practice turning off the automatic pilot on your dialect and speaking in English.

Another strategy can be used when you are being confused yourself by someone else's dialect. Learn to say, "What does that mean?" or, "I do not understand your wording." or any other way of saying, "Please translate for me." Don't be afraid to ask for clarification. Not understanding another tribe's dialect does not mean you are dumb! It only means that you are not a member of that tribe. In many business settings I have often heard the advice, "Never say, 'I don't know,' or, 'I don't understand.'" That is dangerous advice. Not only is it likely to produce a disastrous number of mistakes, it is also likely to damage relationships between tribes in ways that make tribal warfare inevitable.

And finally, be sure to train new employees in the tribal dialects of other companies or industries that they will be in regular contact with. Make up a glossary if necessary. Most companies do a much better job training new employees about internal tribal characteristics and never give a thought to those outside tribes that the new employees will often be talking with.

Values.   If I had to choose the most important tribal characteristic from the five that are described in this book, I would pick values. All tribes are committed to their values and are often quite passionate about them. This is true, of course, for customers as well. If you are not living up to your client's definition of quality, then you are probably in the process of losing a client. Client loyalty because of long-time quality service may keep him with you even if all other characteristics of your tribe and organization change completely.

Listen carefully for your customer's definition of quality. After you know what it is, make sure that you at least match that standard and then, if at all possible, try to surpass it by a mile. When it comes to values, the best companies make a habit of going consistently above and beyond their customer's expectations.

Industries and organizations can define quality quite differently. These different definitions are often a source of conflict between industry tribes. One place where conflict often occurs is between nonprofit and for-profit organizations. In health care, for instance, there are religious hospitals, such as the Catholic systems, and proprietary hospitals run by for-profit corporations. The conflicts between the two groups are evident in their respective dialects. The proprietary hospitals call themselves "investor-owned facilities" and refer to the other kind of hospital as "non-tax–paying facilities." The religious or government hospitals, on the other hand, call themselves "nonprofit facilities" and refer to the other tribe as "the for-profits." This language difference is only the tip of the iceberg of their ongoing tribal conflict.

This same kind of friction occurred when a prestigious university and an equally prestigious major corporation attempted to join forces to provide a service in the region where both institutions were located. The contrast between these two tribes was apparent in both large and small ways. People from either side would come away from planning meetings shaking their heads at the other group's strange, and at times offensive, behavior. One of them said to me at one point, "They don't even *dress* like we do." The pin-stripe three-piece tribe meets the khakis and sports jacket tribe. The project was finally launched, but the turnover rate on both sides has been extremely high.

Anyone who has ever been through a corporate merger or has studied the current literature on corporate culture will know that combining two different organizational cultures into one company can be like mixing oil and water. On a smaller scale, the same oil-and-water phenomenon can occur when two individuals from different companies or industries carry on a conversation, trying to reach a meeting of the minds.

Background and Training.   Construction settings are fertile ground for background and training differences. If a couple is building a house for the first time, it is not likely that their backgrounds and training will be at all similar to those of the crews, the builder, or the architect. Walking onto a building site to encounter carpenters, electricians, plumbers, and a contractor can truly be a trip to Mars for these clients. If the contractor knows how to bridge this gap by finding common background experiences, it will reduce the tension.

A flooring subcontractor I know is famous for being able to find a mutual relative, friend, or school with every customer he meets. The people who work for him laugh and tell me that if he cannot find any background overlap with the customer, it does not slow him down a bit. He just makes something up! This may be extreme, but he is known for his excellent customer relations and service and has a thriving, growing business in a highly competitive field. He knows how to close the gap with the customer.

Thinking Patterns.   The point of listening for your customer's thinking pattern is to match it. Listen for his pacing, and adjust the speed of your own speech accordingly. If he talks concretely, give him facts or stories, not abstractions. When you discover that your customer is a machine-gun thinker, don't drown him in details. But if he is a detail-oriented storyteller, it will not satisfy him if you fire two or three key facts at him and refuse to elaborate. Listen—then migrate!

Rules of the Game.   The customer usually will not see many of your strategies or tactics for getting the job done. There is one rule, however, that he will notice being kept or not: Does the customer come first? Are you on his side? Are you his ally, or his enemy? Are you interested in getting the job done *for him,* or are you more interested in your commission, in your schedule, or even in just getting him off the phone so you can get on to more important matters? The internal tribes have many rules, but customers usually have only one rule: "I come first."

Listening is the Key

Listening and responding to the customer is what matters. The tribal characteristics are useful guides to what you should listen for when a customer is talking. They allow you to migrate toward the customer and to close the gap between his tribe and yours. As discussed in Chapter 8, it is equally important that you make sure the customer *knows* you are listening. When the customer stops talking, say something that lets him know you heard what he just said.

It is essential that you migrate first before you bring the conversation back to your goal. If you do not do this, the customer will end up feeling that you were not listening. Pick any one of the five characteristics to help you acknowledge some piece of what he said in his last statement. Listening to a customer and then responding, "Yeah, yeah . . .," before

Figure 15–1.   Migrating

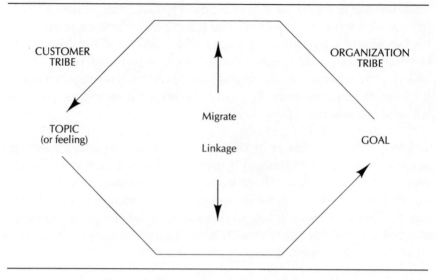

you launch into your own topic is *not* enough. You are asking the customer to assume that you are listening and to trust you. That is a lot to ask. If value is the characteristic you are listening for, say something like, "I understand you are concerned about cost savings. Let me tell you how our service will produce good results for you in that area." That sounds much better to the customer than, "Listen, let me tell you about our service and its benefits to you."

Can you listen too much? In the literature on negotiation strategies, the question is raised of whether you can listen too much and pay too much attention to the other side's perspective. The fear is that by listening too much, you are legitimating the other side's point of view.[1] But a good negotiator will tell you that this is backwards thinking. If you do not make sure that you listen well enough and communicate to the other party that you have listened and understand him, he is not likely to believe that you have heard what he said. When you try to explain your point of view, the other person is going to hear you going off in your own direction with the conversation and will assume that you have not grasped what he just said to you. So he will concentrate on rewording his message and giving it to you again. This repetition can occur over and over until someone ends up angry.

I see salespeople do this all the time with their customers. The customer expresses a concern, or asks a question. Without any acknowledgement of what the customer just said, the salesperson launches into the next point that he wants to make. So the customer tries again. And back comes another response from the salesperson that seems to have no relationship to what the customer just said. After two or three rounds of lopsided conversation, the customer usually gets frustrated and ends the conversation. No sale! Then I ask the salesperson to repeat for me what the customer said in that conversation, and he can repeat it all verbatim. The salesperson *was* listening. So why didn't he *do* anything to let the customer know that?

It may be possible, however, to listen too long in a conversation with a customer. You do not necessarily need to let a very long-winded customer go on and on. The art of interrupting is an important skill in any negotiating or selling situation. But the important thing is what you were doing before you interrupt. If you were listening, and then interrupt to say, "Let me see if I understand what you have been saying to me," the customer will probably respond well to your comments. If you get sick of listening, fog out, and then interrupt to say, "Let me tell you about . . .," you have just lost control of the conversation and damaged your negotiation position.

Contact Overload

In their book, *Service America!*, Karl Albrecht and Ron Zemke talk about "contact overload." Salespeople suffering from this reaction have become "toxic toward their customers."[2] Front line tribes that have a great deal of contact with customers can develop a behavior that they call the "robotization" of the job—the "have a nice day" syndrome.

This behavior usually leads a salesperson into making hostile and combative responses. Front-line tribes are much more likely to fall into this behavior in an organizational atmosphere of intense tribal friction. When employee stress levels are high and there is very little support and migrating between tribes, employees will become worn out more easily. Tribal warfare does not create an environment supportive enough to give employees the energy to go the extra mile for the customer. They are using too much of their time and energy defending their turf.

In my work with customer relations issues in organizations, I have found that you cannot separate treatment of customers from treatment of colleagues. People are not light switches. They cannot turn from a battle with another employee or tribe and, in the next breath, be genuinely responsive and focused on a customer. Improving your internal tribal relations is a crucial element in protecting and improving your customer relations.

OTHER INDUSTRY CONTACTS

Another form of warfare occurs when different industries come in contact with each other. Each industry has its own set of tribes and characteristics and these rarely dovetail smoothly with another industry's pattern of operating.

I have witnessed the banking, insurance, and securities industries trying to talk with each other. Their language, values, backgrounds, thinking, and rules are all different. And yet representatives from each industry must find some way to communicate with each other to get the job done for the customer. With their history of tribal conflict, these three groups often do not have very high opinions of each other. I have had bankers tell me that brokers are "sleazeballs"; brokers tell me that bankers are "tedious bores"; and neither of them have any regard at all for insurance people. This is not a good starting point for effective cross-tribal communication.

Many industries that work together have an unspoken, but well-known, pecking order among their tribes, and this can also cause resentment. In the building industry, for example, it is widely agreed upon that carpenters are at the top of the pecking order among the trades, and that the architects have more status than builders or engineers. On a corporate level, there is the same sort of pecking order among companies within an industry, and between companies in a city. Anyone who works in the corporate world knows that certain companies that are "the place to work" in your industry or city. For a number of years, I worked in one of my city's "hot companies" in its industry. When I left to start my own business, I would offer prospective clients my references and would frequently hear, "Oh, I don't need to check your references. If you came from that company, I know you're good." Having worked, in my opinion, with my fair share of talent and turkeys within that very good company, I was always amazed at their blind confidence. The pecking order highlights the differences between companies, increases competition, and can easily fan the flames of potential conflict.

Pacing Differences

One of the most frustrating gaps between industry tribes is differences in pacing. Some industries and companies operate at much faster speeds than others. This is one of the primary sources of conflict between the banking, insurance, and securities industries. Employees in brokerage firms that handle insurance products have moaned to me many times about being caught in the middle between the brokers and the insurance industry. For example, when a broker decides to be licensed to sell certain insurance products, he fills out the application, takes the test, and is ready to sell— now! The insurance industry, on the other hand, takes four to six weeks to process the application and issue the license. The brokerage firm clerk is caught in the middle between the fast-paced, impatient broker and the slower, procedure-bound insurance industry.

Each organization has its own rhythm and pace. This will vary, of course, to some extent from tribe to tribe within the organization, but there will be a general pattern that everyone understands and follows. When I go into a new industry or company, pacing is one of the first things I investigate. It gives me many quick clues about which tribes are most likely to irritate each other—both within and outside the organization.

I start by asking the following question, and I recommend that you ask it about your own tribe and organization. Even if you have to estimate, your answer will still be useful when you think about your tribe or organization's contact with other industries.

What is the turnaround time on a piece of information in your tribe or organization? In other words, if there is a problem or a need for information, how long do you have to get the answer? A month, a week, a day, five minutes—I have heard all these answers from different tribes. If you have a five-minute tribe in one industry talking to a one-month tribe in another industry, you have potential trouble on your hands. It is important to point out that working in a tribe or industry with a five-minute turnaround time does not necessarily mean that you will necessarily be able to get the answer within five minutes. It means that if you do not get it within five minutes, someone will be yelling in your face about where the answer is. Another way to think about the pacing issue is to ask yourself, how many minutes or days' worth of patience exists in my industry or my company? How quickly does the patience run out here?

When two industries or companies with different paces come into contact, neither is likely to change to accommodate the other. Usually the only strategy that is available to you as a representative of one of them is to be as specific about time lines as possible and to persuade the other tribal representative to speed up or slow down as much as he can within his tribe's pacing range (not yours). So if you need a response from a slower paced industry, do not accept "as soon as possible" as an adequate answer. Those words mean entirely different things to your two tribes. If you push for a specific time line and get the answer "four to six weeks," negotiate for four weeks and try to get that commitment. Trying to negotiate for a one-week response in this case is probably useless, unless you know that other companies in their industry have faster time lines and that you can go elsewhere for the same service at a faster speed. Often, however, the other companies in that industry are going to be operating in the four-to-six-week time frame as well.

If you are the representative of the slower tribe, you can reduce the frequency of the angry follow-up calls you receive if you quit giving vague, noncommittal time lines. You say, "It will be there soon," meaning two to three weeks, but they hear "soon" as three to four days. You are begging to get yelled at by the end of the week.

One of the interesting spin-offs of pacing differences between companies and industries is that capitalizing on them can open new markets. If your industry operates at a two-week turnaround time for a product, service, or solution, and you can find a way to reduce that pace to one week or three days, you have differentiated your product in a significant and potentially marketable way. If, however, the industry your tribe is trying to communicate with is the federal government, the IRS, or some other slower paced tribe, it is not likely to be motivated by a new-market–niche mentality. Learning to recognize and live with the pacing differences is often your only option.

Changing Industry Tribes

Moving from one industry to another can be as disorienting in many ways as moving from one country to another. It requires that you break old tribal affiliations and form new ones. This is usually not a quick or painless process. Moving from one department to another within a company requires learning new language, values, rules, and so on, but these differences in tribal characteristics are usually seen as more dramatic when changing industries.

The pacing difference alone is a major adjustment. If you move into a slower industry, you may suffer from boredom and restlessness. You may also be accused of being pushy and too aggressive and impatient. On the other hand, moving into a fast-paced industry may leave you feeling as though you are constantly racing but never quite catching up. You may be in danger of being seen as not bright enough, as too disorganized, or as a "loser." Once these reputations are formed, they take a long time to overcome.

Learning as much as possible about a new industry before you make the move will help, but many of the subtler parts of tribal behavior cannot be learned until you live with them. Probably the best strategy for safely surviving the transition is to admit that you do not know the lay of the land in this new company, but that you are willing to learn and learn fast. Listening, asking questions, and seeking advice will give you a great deal of information and will also send the signal that you respect the new tribe and are interested in being a member.

QUESTIONS TO ASK ABOUT CUSTOMER AND OTHER INDUSTRY TRIBES

What jargon words does your customer use repeatedly? What do these words mean to him? Gary Goodman, author of *Winning by Telephone*, calls these words "personalisms."[3] If you can pick up on these words, use them—or at least do not keep contradicting him in the conversation. Many "experts" are tempted to correct their customers in their inaccurate word usage. At times this may be important to do, but be careful. Your customer's language is as important to him as yours is to you.

What is the most important thing about your product or service to your typical customer? What is your customer's definition of quality? How can you at least match that definition, or even better, surpass the customer's standards? If you want a very loyal customer, values are the area to concentrate on when developing the relationship. Consistency is important in this area. If on-time delivery and accurate billing procedures are components of your customer's definition of quality service, an occasional on-time delivery and bills that are accurate three months out of four are not good enough. When it comes to values, customers will want consistent and predictable behavior from you.

Is your customer's training and background similar to yours? If not, how can you bridge the gap between you? What kinds of translations or explanations does your customer need from you to feel comfortable doing business with you? Physicians are the classic example. Some doctors do an excellent job of bridging the gap and treating their patients as though they are intelligent members of some other tribe. Other doctors, however, treat patients in ways that communicate that they think the patients either have very low IQ levels or are entirely too irritating to even try to communicate with about technical matters. Those are the physicians who are losing patients at increasingly rapid rates and are even being sued more frequently. Bridging the gap between your tribe and your customer's tribe is important for developing of trust as well as loyalty.

Is the pace of your customer's thinking and talking fast or slow? Try to adjust your pace to match your customer's pace. Is talking in facts, or in stories and images? Is he talking in details, or in "big-picture" summaries? Try to migrate and match your customer's pattern of thinking and talking as closely as you can.

Remember that the main rule for any customer is, "The customer comes first." *What does your customer expect by that?* What are the things that you can do to indicate to him that he comes first to you, at least at moment you are talking? Focusing on the customer you are talking with at the time is a very important aspect of this rule. If you are talking to a customer, but really thinking about where else you need to be or who else you need to call next, the customer will sense it. Your mind is in Bolivia, and he knows it! *Concentrate* on the customer you are talking to now. Shotgun thinking and scattered concentration are the fastest ways to communicate that a customer does not come first to you.

Have any of your internal tribes become "toxic" to your customers? If some of your tribes have high levels of customer contact and are under a great deal of pressure to perform quickly and politely, they are prime candidates for contact overload. They can become hostile, or just plain numb. This, of course, is not the kind of behavior that will bridge the gap effectively between your organization and its customers. Rotating people, rewarding them, hiring people with high customer tolerance, and stress management training are all strategies that you can use to try to reduce this problem.

Do you do anything to train your employees in the language, values, thinking, backgrounds, and rules of the noncustomer external tribes that they have regular contact with? You're the exception to the rule if you do. Usually this learning only takes place once the employees are on the job and actually having to communicate with these outside groups. The message they learn from their experience and from the comments of their fellow tribal members is usually not one of tolerance. Instead they learn that those other guys are "idiots" or some other more colorful descriptor. Tribal warfare can happen outside the borders of your organization as easily as it can happen inside. Bridging the gap with your other industry contacts is usually well worth the effort.

There is no one reality. We have all heard that before, but the usefulness of that statement usually escapes us. This book has taken a practical look at all the different realities that you work with everyday, in the tribes both inside and outside of your organization. The tribes may never truly understand each other, and they are certainly not likely to ever agree with each other. But as this book has attempted to demonstrate, it is possible to have tribal peace whether or not the tribes understand or agree with each other.

Contact between tribes is inevitable, but warfare is not. With an understanding of the different benefits that all your tribes bring to your organization, and with the development of the skills to negotiate and bridge tribal gaps, employees can transform tribal warfare into peaceful, productive tribal relationships—which produce better results for everyone.

NOTES

CHAPTER 1: TRIBES IN CONFLICT

1. Tom Jones, "Managing Corporate Conflict," *Today's Office* (November 1983): 51; and Gordon Lippett, Ronald Lippit, and Clayton Luffbuty, "Cutting Edge Trends in OD," *Training and Development Journal* (July 1984): 60.
2. Edward T. Hall, *Beyond Culture* (New York: Doubleday/Anchor , 1976), p. 43.
3. Lealand R. Kaiser, "Organizational Mindset: Ten Ways to 'Alter Your World View,'" *Healthcare Forum* (January-February 1986): 50.
4. Hall, *Beyond Culture,* p. 43.
5. Clive Rassam, "How to Solve Interdepartmental Conflict," *International Management* (October 1976): 47.
6. Quoted in Gerald I. Nierenberg, *Fundamentals of Negotiating* (New York: Harper and Row, 1987), p. 22.
7. Ibid.

CHAPTER 2: CHARACTERISTICS OF ORGANIZATIONAL TRIBES

1. Philip Kotler, *Marketing Management: Analysis, Planning and Control,* 4th ed. (Englewood Cliffs, N.J.: Prentice-Hall, 1980), p. 595.

2. Ibid.
3. Robert H. Waterman, Jr., *The Renewal Factor: How the Best Get and Keep the Competitive Edge* (New York: Bantam, 1987), p. 183.
4. Hall, *Beyond Culture,* p. 133.
5. Jan Carlzon, *Moments of Truth* (Cambridge, Mass.: Ballinger, 1987), p.84.
6. Ned Herrmann, "The Creative Brain," *Training and Development Journal* (October 1981): 13.
7. Hall, *Beyond Culture,* p. 32.
8. Kotler, *Marketing Management,* p. 595.

CHAPTER 3: TRIBAL LANGUAGES AND DIALECTS

1. Hall, *Beyond Culture,* p. 132.
2. Suzette Haden Elgin, *The Last Word on The Gentle Art of Verbal Self-Defense* (New York: Prentice-Hall, 1987), p.156.
3. Elgin, *The Gentle Art,* p. 156.
4. Gary S. Goodman, *Winning by Telephone: Telephone Effectiveness for the Business Man and Consumer* (Englewood Cliffs, N.J.: Prentice-Hall, 1982), p. 30.
4. Ibid, p. 29.

CHAPTER 4: TRIBAL VALUES

1. Charles A. Garfield, *Peak Performers: The New Heroes of American Business* (New York: Avon, 1987), p. 87.
2. Waterman, *Renewal Factor,* p. 11.
3. Ibid., p. 12.
4. Tom Peters and Nancy Austin, *A Passion for Excellence: The Leadership Difference* (New York: Random House, 1985), p. 83.
5. Carlzon, *Moments of Truth,* p. 67.
6. Waterman, *Renewal Factor,* p. 90
7. Charles M. Kelly, "The Interrelationship of Ethics and Power in Today's Organizations," *Organizational Dynamics* (1987):15.
8. Garfield, *Peak Performers*, p. 23.
9. Waterman, *Renewal Factor,* p. 193
10. Alfie Kohn, "How to Succeed Without Even Vying," *Psychology Today,* (September 1986): 24.
11. Peters and Austin, *Passion for Excellence,* p. 101.
12. Ibid.
13. Janice M. Beyer and Harrison Price, "How an Organization's Rites Reveal

Its Culture," *Organizational Dynamics,* 15(Spring 1987): 23.
14.   Waterman, *Renewal Factor,* p. 11.
15.   Steven Brandt, *Entrepreneuring in Established Companies: Managing Toward the Year 2000* (Homewood, Ill.: Dow Jones-Irwin, 1985), p. 100.

CHAPTER 5: TRIBAL TRAINING

1.   From "The Uniqueness Paradox in Organizational Stories" by Joanne Martin, Martha S. Feldman, Mary Jo Hatch, and Sim B. Sitkin, *Administrative Science Quarterly* 28, no. 3 (September 1983): 144, 441-445, © 1983 Cornell University. Reprinted by permission of *Administrative Science Quarterly.*

CHAPTER 6: TRIBAL THINKING PATTERNS

1.   Ned Herrmann, lecture given at the Whole Brain Corporation Certification Seminar, Ashville, NC, 1984.
2.   Ned Herrmann, "The Creative Brain", *Training and Development Journal* (October 1981).
3.   Isabel Briggs Myers and Peter B. Myers, *Gifts Differing* (Palo Alto, Cal.: Consulting Psychological Press, 1980).
4.   Herrmann, lecture
5.   Suzette Haden Elgin, *The Last Word on the Gentle Art of Verbal Self-Defense* (Englewood Cliffs, N.J.: Prentice-Hall, 1987) p. 67.
6.   The diagnostic also draws on the work of Isabel Briggs Myers and Ned Herrmann. See note 4. There is a similar survey in Jacquelyn Wonder and Priscilla Donovan, *Whole-Brain Thinking: Working from Both Sides of the Brain to Achieve Peak Job Performance* (New York: Morrow, 1984), p. 31.

CHAPTER 7: TRIBAL RULES OF THE GAME

1.   Gifford Pinchot, *Intrapreneuring* (New York: Harper and Row, 1985), p. 198.

CHAPTER 8: MIGRATING SKILLS

1.   Janice M. Beyer and Harrison M. Trice, "How an Organization's Rites Reveal Its Culture," *Organizational Dynamics* (1987): 16.

2.   Fred Jandt and Paul Gillette, *Win-Win Negotiating: Turning Conflicts into Agreement* (New York: John Wiley & Sons, 1985).

CHAPTER 9: SKILLS FOR HANDLING TRIBAL STRESS

1.   Robert Kriegel and Marilyn Harms Kriegel, *The C Zone: Peak Performance Under Pressure* (New York: Doubleday/Anchor, 1984), p. 49.
2.   Salvatore R. Maddi and Suzanne C. Kobasa, *The Hardy Executive: Health Under Stress,* (Homewood, Ill.: Dow Jones-Irwin, 1984), p. 31.
3.   James Loehr, speech given at the Denver Center for Athletic Excellence, Wheat Ridge, Colorado.
4.   Kriegel and Kriegel, *C Zone*, p. 60.
5.   Maddi and Kobasa, *Hardy Executive*, p. 31
6.   Kriegel and Kriegel, *C Zone,* p. 85.

CHAPTER 11: INNOVATION

1.   Michael Kirton, "Adaption-Innovation: A Theory of Organizational Creativity," in Stanley S. Gryskiewicz and James T. Shields, eds., *Creativity Week IV: 1981 Proceedings* (Greensboro, N.C.: Center for Creative Leadership, 1982), p. 93.
2.   Ibid.
3.   Pinchot, *Intrapreneuring*, p. xv.
4.   Marian B. McLeod, "The Communication Problems of Scientists in Business and Industry," *Journal of Business Communication* (Spring 1978): 27.
5.   Quoted in McLeod, "Communication Problems," p. 29.
6.   Pinchot, *Intrapreneuring*, p. 187.
7.   Peter Drucker, *Innovation and Entrepreneurship: Practice and Principles* (New York: Harper and Row, 1985), p. 138.
8.   Ibid.

CHAPTER 13: TRIBAL ETHICS

1.   "A Question of Ethics," *Wall Street Journal,* 18 September 1987.
2.   Robert F. Allen, "The IK in the Office," *Organizational Dynamics,* (Winter 1980): 30..

3. Ibid., p. 31.
4. Irving Kristol, "Ethics, Anyone? Or Morals?" *Wall Street Journal,* 15 September 1987.
5. Ibid.
6. Robert Bellah, *Habits of the Heart: Individualism and Commitment in American Life* (New York: Harper and Row, 1986).
7. Sir Adrian Cadbury, "Ethical Managers Make Their Own Rules," *Harvard Business Review* (September-October 1987): 69.
8. Ibid., p. 71.
9. Manual Velasquez, Dennis J. Moberg, and Gerald F. Cavanaugh, "Organizational Statesmanship and Dirty Politics: Ethical Guidelines for the Organizational Politician," *Organizational Dynamics* (Autumn 1983): 67.
10. Allen, "IK in the Office," p.33.

CHAPTER 15: CUSTOMER TRIBES AND OTHER INDUSTRY TRIBES

1. Roger Fisher and William Ury, *Getting to Yes, Negotiating Agreement Without Giving in* (Boston: Houghton Mifflin, 1981), p. 35.
2. Karl Albrecht and Ron Zemke, *Service America! Doing Business in the New Economy* (Homewood, Ill.: Dow Jones-Irwin, 1985), p. 101.
3. Goodman, *Winning by Telephone,* p. 9.

ABOUT THE AUTHOR

Peg C. Neuhauser is a communications consultant who specializes in working with business in the areas of team building and conflict management. She is the owner and principal consultant of PCN ASSOCIATES in Nashville, Tennessee.

Ms. Neuhauser has published a number of articles in business and professional journals. In addition, she speaks regularly on topics related to team building, innovation, managing change in organizations, and negotiation skills. Her clients include major American corporations from industries such as manufacturing, health care, finance, and telecommunications.

For information about services provided by PCN ASSOCIATES, please call or write:

Peg C. Neuhauser
PCN ASSOCIATES
1413 Calvin Avenue
Nashville, TN 37206
615-377-9720